STUDIES IN ROMANCE LANGUAGES: 3

THE LITERARY WORLD OF

Ana Maria Matute

by Margaret E. W. Jones

The University Press of Kentucky
Lexington   1970

863.64
J 72 L
74110
april, 1971

Standard Book Number: 8131–1228–1

Library of Congress Catalog Card Number: 77–119813

Copyright © 1970 by The University Press of Kentucky

A statewide cooperative scholarly publishing agency serving Berea
College, Centre College of Kentucky, Eastern Kentucky University,
Kentucky State College, Morehead State University, Murray State
University, University of Kentucky, University of Louisville, and
Western Kentucky University.

Editorial and Sales Offices: Lexington, Kentucky 40506

for

Molly,

Teddy,

&

Julie Anne

Contents

Acknowledgments

I would like to thank Professors E. R. Mulvihill and A. Sánchez-Barbudo for their helpful suggestions during the preparation of the original manuscript; the Kentucky Research Foundation, for funds made available for the present study; and John Paul Boyd, Karen Austin, Kathleen Greene, and especially Mrs. Celinda Todd, for their time in typing and proofreading. Special thanks go to my husband for his patient help, constructive criticism, and encouragement.

Introduction

Ana María Matute holds a place of prominence among the greatest contemporary writers of Spain. Her works, which now include eight novels and nine collections of short stories, sketches, and essays, have won the Premio de la Crítica, the Premio Nacional de Literatura, and the Premio Nadal, to mention the most prestigious. Translations of her works into many languages and recent editions of her books for American classroom use have assured her of a wide non-Spanish public.

Although her literature is not consistently autobiographical, there are clear points of contact between her life and her works, a fact which she has often acknowledged. In the chapters which follow, I have indicated autobiographical elements where I think they illuminate Ana María Matute's creative process or explain an obscure passage. But the brief biography below may help orient the reader who is less familiar with modern Spanish culture and history.

Ana María Matute was born in 1926, the second of five children.[1] Her father was a Catalan industrialist, and for business reasons her family lived in both Barcelona and Madrid, spending the summers in Mansilla de la Sierra (Castilla la Vieja), where the mother had some property. Because of these moves, she had a sense of not belonging: in Madrid, she was the *catalana*; in Barcelona, the *castellana*.

She herself has described the sheltered life of her childhood: "The education received by the children of this [middle] class in pre-Civil War Spain generally kept them separate, distant from that world which did not consist of family and intimate friends. Nearly all of us attended a religious boarding school. In those years religious education, especially for girls, was extremely isolated and shut off from the world, which was pictured as something distant, atrocious, terribly dangerous, diabolical and corrupting."[2]

When she was eight, a year spent with her grandparents in Castilla la Vieja disabused her of innocent ideas: the sight of children pulling on the plow after having sold their horse to buy seed, and women plowing with their children tied to their backs, showed that life could be hard and cruel, and that injustice existed. The outbreak of the Civil War in 1936, when Ana María was ten, reinforced this impression: "Suddenly we were shown, with all its crudeness, that 'atrocious' world, that world which had been damned for us in advance."[3] These experiences were to mark the tone and orientation of her literature.

She was a precocious child with an early vocation for literature; she wrote short stories and illustrated them herself, and produced plays in her toy puppet theater. Although she studied painting and music, she soon realized that she preferred writing, a profession to which she dedicated herself early in life. Since her first serious work at age sixteen, Miss Matute has continued to produce novels, short stories, essays, and books for children at a rapid rate.

In 1952, she married the novelist Ramón Eugenio de Goicoechea and bore him a son (Juan Pablo) in 1954; they were divorced in 1963.

Ana María Matute has had a surprising success in this country, considering the fact that her public is limited. She has been visiting lecturer at Indiana University and has given several lecture tours in the United States. She is a corresponding member of the Hispanic Society of America, and recently Mungar Memorial Library of Boston University has instituted the Ana María Matute collection, which consists of several original manuscripts, many with drawings by the author.

Those who tend to classify the new writers by stylistic or thematic affinities have placed Matute within a group characterized by a preference for realism and critical intentions of a moral and social nature.[4] Several critics have as well conceded her an extremely important place within this generation: "At the head of the novelists of the present decade I would place one man and one woman. The woman is Ana María Matute."[5] Others echo this praise in proclaiming her the best woman writer of her generation.[6] A fundamental reason for her popularity is the peculiarly subjective stamp which all of her literature bears. The phrases *estilo personal* and *mundo interior* appear with regularity in analyses of her works, and several critics have investigated elements of this personal novelistic world.[7]

The basis of this "world" is Ana María Matute's interpretation of life, discernible in the reactions of her characters. Her personal philosophy motivates the characters, colors the descriptions, and dictates the mode of expression. Part of this original outlook is a marked division between each of the periods of life: childhood, adolescence, and adulthood. The separation is so germane to her literature that I have followed her own ideological division by discussing her conception of these periods and the major themes developed within them. Through an analysis of these three stages of life, the reader will discover the recurrent types and ideas which so clearly illustrate Ana María Matute's personal reactions, translated into fiction.

A discussion treating of ideological cross-sections and recurrent themes calls for a qualitative analysis, avoiding the unnecessary repetitions of the chronological approach. My study, therefore, presupposes an acquaintance with the plots; for this reason, the first chapter is intended mainly for the reader who has been attracted by one or two of Matute's works and wishes to see them all in chronological setting or to acquaint himself with the basic lines of her complete production; it presents plot and stylistic and thematic elements in order of publication. Such an overall view is also helpful in showing the direction of the author's interests; but the reader familiar enough with Matute's fiction may turn directly to chapter 2.

1. The Works of Ana María Matute

Ana María Matute's debut into the literary world attracted considerable attention: *Los Abel*, published in 1948,[1] received high honors from the Nadal committee that year.[2] As an early work, it reveals much of a young writer's inexperience, but it also includes most of the important themes that Matute has exploited in her later works. The title suggests the basic plot line: a reinterpretation of the Cain and Abel motif, as the Biblical tragedy recurs in modern times, in a family bearing the fated name. The memoirs of the oldest daughter Valba Abel (found by a relative in the now deserted Abel house) provide the reader with a detailed picture of the disintegration of the family. Seven brothers and sisters and the widowed father live in the same house, but familiarity does not necessarily include understanding or harmony. Their apparent togetherness masks a struggle for separateness, with each trying to assert himself, all in conflict because of varied goals and personalities. The drama finally centers around Aldo, who feels the pull of the land and is brusque, hard-working, and insensitive to the feelings of others, and Tito, the favored one. Like the Biblical Abel, Tito seems blessed in what he does, and he accepts bad luck with nonchalance. As the story progresses, the family slowly separates and several go to the city, which becomes the locale of the second half of the work.

The rivalry between Tito and Aldo for the love of Jacqueline sets the inevitable tragedy in motion. The girl is in love with Tito, but marries Aldo and makes him leave his home when she learns of an affair between Tito and her mother. Tito then returns to the village to experiment with modern agricultural techniques; his easy success infuriates Aldo. Valba's story heightens this tense state of affairs: rejecting the uninspiring love offered by Eloy, the town doctor, she also escapes to the city to experience life intensely. Her involvement with an older man soon ends with his desertion. A failure, she returns home, soon followed by Aldo, whose inability to adjust to city life and subsequent abandonment by Jacqueline send him back to the family place. Taunted by his brother about his ill-fated marriage, enraged at Tito's apparent good fortune in whatever he undertakes, Aldo shoots him. The story ends as Valba wets her face with her brother's blood, "como si fuera una caricia" (p. 227).

A penetrating psychological study of Valba—her first awakening to an adult world, her efforts to balance her ideals with reality—initiates Ana María Matute's exploration of man's inevitable necessity of compromise and eventual disillusionment. She introduces other themes which reappear consistently in later works: the inexorable passage of time, the dehumanization of the individual, the solitude of man, and the Cain and Abel motif. These themes, however, do not appear to great advantage in *Los Abel;* as soon as the characters are transplanted to the alien atmosphere of the city, they become, as J. L. Cano states, "muñecos de trapo . . . que no nos convencen. Dejamos de amarlos y cerramos el libro pensando que se ha frustrado una gran novela."[3] The tense psychological interaction is at its best in the country because there the brothers are physically together yet mentally isolated from each other. When each goes his own way, the author fails to maintain this artistic tension. The attitude of the village complements the Abel drama: undercurrents of tension and animallike brutality couple with descriptions of violent aspects of nature to provide an appropriate background for the tragedy of the family; amid the concrete sidewalks and tall buildings of the city the conflicts ring false.

The *memoria,* a form which Matute uses effectively, offers

a triple perspective by juxtaposing three stages of time: the present tense (discarded as soon as the memoirs are opened) of the peruser of Valba's notes; Valba's own comments as she ponders the events she is describing, separated from them by the passage of time; and finally, the story itself, which is written in the past tense. These layers of time fuse in Valba's present outlook. The bitter hopelessness of her tone as she writes leaves no doubt as to a tragic ending.

Exclamations of despair and horror as well as frequent self-questioning punctuate the relatively simply prose style. Repeated references to the more violent or unreceptive forms of nature, a stress on the color red, the sharp contrast of light and dark, a distorting focus occasionally directed toward certain objects are stylistic devices to complement Valba's unhappiness.

Fiesta al noroeste (1952), Ana María Matute's first prize-winning work,[4] describes the abnormal attraction of Juan Medinao toward his half-brother Pablo, and the resultant effects on Juan's personality. The book opens as the puppeteer Dingo returns to his native town, La Artámila, accidentally runs over a little boy, is detained by the police, and calls on the powerful landowner Juan Medinao for aid. Dingo and Juan had been childhood friends and had once saved money to escape together from La Artámila; Dingo had later disappeared with their joint savings to join a company of travelling actors.

A priest, brought in for the funeral of the little boy, also hears Juan's general confession. Each chapter of the novel, framed by the confession of another sin, tells of Juan's lonely existence. He is ugly and unpopular, and has found in religion both a consolation and a defense. When one of the family servants, Salomé, bears Juan's illegitimate half-brother Pablo, Juan's life changes completely. Fascinated by his own ambivalent mixture of attraction and repulsion, Juan tries to win Pablo's favor. Even though, years later, Pablo leads a strike against Juan for higher wages (which ultimately fails), Juan still ineffectually tries by every means (even marrying Pablo's fiancée) to keep his half-brother at his side. All his attempts are unsuccessful; Pablo finally leaves for the city. Powerless either to retain or to dominate Pablo, Juan rapes Salomé, Pablo's mother, in a final gesture of despair and triumph.

The liberal use of Catholic elements in *Fiesta al noroeste* has tempted one critic to suggest that Ana María Matute failed in an effort to produce an "authentic Catholic novel."[5] Although she does not intend to orient *Fiesta al noroeste* in the direction suggested by this critic, Matute uses religious practices to best novelistic advantage: the confession as a framework for Juan's story ironically underscores the unchristian basis of his fanatical devotion. It is an obvious but perfectly adapted narrative device for allowing Juan to reveal himself and his past.

Juan Medinao is a twisted and ingrown person—in the words of his half-brother, *podrido* (p. 110); instead of accepting life, he rejects it out of false piety. He rationalizes his own failures in coping with reality and convinces himself that his rejection is based on ethical principles. He is strongly attracted toward Pablo because his half-brother represents an attitude toward life unknown to Juan: freedom and the unhesitating acceptance of life. These two characters reenact a modern version of the story of Cain and Abel, introduced previously with the symbolic Abel family. Each man personifies opposite sides of a single personality: the "Abel" of the story, Pablo, is vigorous, healthy, and untroubled by life; Juan —"Cain"—is weak, deformed, and haunted by problems which he cannot solve. Of the two men, Juan is by far the more interesting; Pablo's almost smug complacency is an intentional stylization of character to provide the necessary contrast and background against which "Cain's" drama will be played. Traditional realism is discarded here in favor of a descriptive technique which adapts the mood of the novel to that of the main character by distorting basically realistic characters and surroundings.

The protagonists move through a stylized landscape peculiar to Ana María Matute's writing, which has more than once been compared with the equally grotesque world of Solana's paintings.[6] The setting reflects the desolation of the characters in the emphasis on menacing aspects of nature made strange by personification. The author's comments on *Fiesta al noroeste* reaffirm the intimate ties between land, atmosphere, and characters: "Si la acción sucede en Castilla—y ello se presupone aunque no se diga de un modo concreto . . . —no es por un azar cualquiera. . . . Esa Castilla [la Vieja] es, aun hoy, el acervo de un tiempo, de un clima mental, de un modo de ser, donde las pasiones cualesquiera se dan en estado primigenio."[7]

Certain technical advances are apparent in *Fiesta al noroeste*. To the simple prose of *Los Abel*, the author adds strange sensorial images and rich metaphorical expressions, devices which mark a turning point to a more ornate mode of composition. Similes from nature ("estaba ya muy quieto como sorprendido de amapolas" [p. 13]), modern conceits, such as blood compared to flowers of impossible strength ("fuerza imposible" [p. 34]), or ironic metaphors ("A tres gatos . . . el sol les ponía aureola y parecían santitos" [p. 128]) echo the definite insistence on a poetic distortion of reality.

Fiesta al noroeste is an excellent example of the subordination of plot to the study of man; the action generally serves as a pretext for exploring some facet of human nature or behavior. Dingo's return sets in motion a chain of events which culminates in the flashback confession of Juan. The latter discloses the real subject of the novel through his talks with the priest: the desolation of a man who is doomed to failure in his attempt to solve his problems. The atmosphere of anxiety and mental torture, the tension sustained throughout the work and the expressionistic deformation of the landscape are all projections of Juan's wretched state of mind. Thus the second of Matute's variations on the theme of Cain and Abel barely touches on Abel's story in the preference given to Cain's strange drama.

The role of Dingo as a puppeteer merits some comment here, for it introduces another constant theme in the novelist's works and one which contributes greatly to the stylization of the novels: the *grand guignol* aspect of life. In her remarks about *Fiesta al noroeste,* the author affirms this interest on her part: "Este cerco trágico y áspero del gran 'guignol' que a veces es el cerco de la vida"; "Juan Medinao es una pobre máscara."[8] In this novel, however, the idea of "all the world's a stage" is only an accessory theme; it is in *Pequeño teatro,* her next novel, that the real merits and defects of this theme as the basis of a whole work will have to be weighed.

Ana María Matute received the Premio Editorial Planeta for *Pequeño teatro* (1954), though it is inferior in many respects to the novels she published both before and after this date. It is her third published book, but the seeming retrogression is due to the fact that *Pequeño teatro* is actually her first literary work, written when she was eighteen.[9]

Her preference for rural settings continues in this novel, although the locale moves from inland to Oiquixa, an imaginary fishing town on the Basque coast.[10] The town's small size seems to encourage the pettiness of the inhabitants, whose boredom makes them seize on anything that will entertain. Gossip is the main diversion, an occupation passed from mother to daughter. Thus the arrival of Marco on the scene constitutes a big event, and his grandiloquent speech and impressive air blind everyone to the truth that he is only a penniless adventurer. The only person not duped is Zazu, the unhappy adolescent daughter of the powerful but equally unhappy Kepa. Zazu's nymphomaniac tendencies, the scandal of Oiquixa, tempt Marco to capture her heart and then abandon her. His other project intrigues the citizens of Oiquixa even more: he takes charge of Ilé, a disreputable and neglected orphan, because, according to Marco, the boy is a genius. The townspeople use Ilé as a pawn to curry Marco's favor. The domineering Eskarne and her timid sister Mirentxu lead the group in showering the boy with attention, even offering to share the burden of Ilé's upbringing with Marco, who cleverly suggests a "Gran Colecta pro Futuro Genio de Oiquixa." The rest of the story is easy to foresee. The day after the *colecta*, Marco is ready to set sail. Zazu, fighting against her fatal attraction toward him, drowns herself. The spell is broken; Marco is exposed and put in jail; Ilé is once again left uncared for.

The leitmotif of this work, briefly alluded to in previous books, is that of "life is a stage," or as the critic Castellet states, "En una palabra [Oiquixa es] uno de tantos 'pequeños teatros' cuya agrupación forma el Gran Teatro del Mundo."[11] The association of the protagonists with the marionettes in the town theater effectively underlines this theme and suggests a magical double reflection of life, systematically confusing the characters and puppets through repeated comparisons.

Balancing the dreamlike atmosphere of the marionette show (represented by the puppeteer Andrea and the pompous Marco) is the reality of Oiquixa. Marco is jailed for his swindle, but the townspeople are also guilty of ethical subterfuge: their charitable display of interest in Ilé is completely false, since it is only a ruse to attract Marco's attention. Ilé is the innocent pawn of the two worlds, and as such, is hurt by both: he is finally abandoned by both Marco and the good citizens of Oiquixa, once they realize that he can no longer be of use to them. However, the suggestive idea of 'all the world's a stage' does not compensate for certain defects in the novel. The atmosphere is so fantastic, the motives of the protagonists so poorly justified, that even the comparison of the townspeople with the puppets does not seem sufficient to explain their irrational actions. J. L. Cano excuses this defect by saying, "Sus virtudes no residen en el interés de la acción y en la fuerza de las pasiones, sino en la belleza del estilo y en la gracia poética."[12] Others have not been so kind. One critic wasted no words condemning it, especially the creation of the characters: "*Pequeño teatro* posee un desequilibrio aún mayor porque la autora navega entre dos aguas: la de una realidad amasada con ese pulso peculiar y la de otra 'realidad objetiva' que no consigue retratar satisfactoriamente. . . . Sus personajes carecen de la necesaria consistencia objetiva y no están tampoco lo bastante 'inventados' para ser una creación. A veces parecen estar dotados de una poetización alegórica, trascendente y se dispeñan luego en una trivialidad mal apresada."[13] One must remember that as the first work of the novelist, it shows an understandable lack of the polish that she later acquired. On the other hand, a skillful handling of language seems to have marked her talents from the first. Poetic passages, the use of synesthesia, and a stress on colors add a lyrical tone which offsets in great part the "triviality" mentioned by Alborg; her attack on false charity—a subject to which she devotes special attention—gives her work a more serious tone than most critics have allowed.

Each of Ana María Matute's works up to this point deliberately obscured any references to a definite time or setting. *En esta tierra* inaugurates a series of novels which break the previous pattern. These post-1956 novels are definitely contemporary in time, with the Civil War used as background material or directly affecting the lives of the characters. The settings of these novels are generally identifiable; *En esta tierra* takes place in Barcelona.

The atmosphere of tension and unease is a major factor in this novel; the Civil War reveals truths about characters that would have remained hidden in less troubled times, as well as insights into human behavior in the eternal conflict between generations, between egotism and unselfishness, between dreams and reality. Soledad and her brother Eduardo find their comfortable, stable existence shattered by the outbreak of the Civil War and the murder of their industrialist father. The economic situation forces them to live a life of privation; part of their house is requisitioned to provide quarters for a low-class Madrid family, including a girl, Cloti, of Soledad's age. Soledad tries to help the family by taking a job with a former tutor, but Eduardo rejects his responsibilities to join a gang led by Daniel, a tubercular boy from the lower class. Fighting his fear of death, Eduardo convinces his sister to accompany him to his dying friend's home. There she meets Daniel's brother Cristián, and after a bombing which kills the rest of the family—the father and Pablo, the eldest son—Soledad and Cristián become lovers and live in Pablo's apartment until they are arrested.

After her release, Soledad knows she is pregnant, finds Cristián in the outskirts of the city, and convinces him to come home with her. As they start toward the highway to Barcelona, they see the *nacionales* approaching; Cristián runs toward them, shouting, and is shot down.

Intercalated in the main body of the novel is a flashback of Pablo's life, which he remembers in the few hours before he dies. A happy childhood abruptly ends when he is forced to work in a slaughterhouse. Through great sacrifice, he manages to become a teacher, but he falls into the apathy of the townspeople he is sent to help. After his transfer to a factory town, he leads an angry group of people in one of the first local manifestations of the revolution. Clearly he is fighting to avenge the injustices he suffered as a boy, but bloodshed does not provide the solution for him. Even after returning to Barcelona to work actively with the *republicanos,* he is restless and dissatisfied. As Pablo dies, he realizes that although Soledad and Cristián may reach the Promised Land which he had envisaged, he will never be permitted to enter.

Obvious personality differences appear in the pairs Cristián-Eduardo and Soledad-Cloti. Idealism and disinterest contrast with cynicism and a selfishness born of deprivation. Pablo and his father, representing the older generation, are the typically embittered adults of Matute's novels. Noteworthy in all these characters are their mental states, ranging from unease to anguish, compared with and complemented by the encompassing war.

Both Soledad and Cristián are adolescents who are isolated from the others, ideologically and even physically. Their motivations, often only half-suggested, have prompted the following comment about Cristián: "No se vislumbraba claramente . . . el fluir y concretarse de sus ideas."[14] In effect, Cristián's gesture at the end of the novel is puzzling. Soledad appears in much the same ambiguous light. Sharply contrasting with the vague characterization of Soledad and Cristián is the more detailed story of Pablo, whose unhappy childhood and frustrated adulthood end in a hopelessness which recalls the Biblical despair of Moses.

Stylistically, the author avoids the original imagery of *Fiesta al noroeste* and *Pequeño teatro.* J. L. Alborg accuses her of a "cierta altisonancia . . . cierta exageración declamatoria que no siempre se excusa por la pasión evidente que pone la escritora en los personajes y peripecias que describe," and refers to the "*tonelaje* de los vocablos, demasiado abultados, excesivamente chillones."[15] The heavy-handed use of adjectives and the *brochazo violento* are part of the writer's attempts to translate this troubled atmosphere into an equally startling vocabulary. It is noteworthy that the only other book in which she employs violent descriptions so liberally is *Los hijos muertos*, which also makes extensive use of the Civil War.

The appearance of *Los niños tontos* once more attested to Ana María Matute's originality, intriguing her readers with its completely different literary approach. Here she discards the format of the novel in favor of twenty-one short sketches in which she deals exclusively with children. The content also deviates radically from that of the novels, for each story is generally a fantasy related in strangely obscure style. A description of some representative sketches will provide an idea of the unusual tone of the work:

"El corderito pascual": A lonely child receives a lamb from his father. He and his pet become inseparable companions. On Easter day, as the family is eating the traditional lamb, he runs out to the kitchen and sees the severed head of his friend.

"El encendio": A boy draws a picture of a fire with his crayons and is burned to death.

"El tiovivo": A child who has no money goes for a ride on a merry-go-round which is closed down. In the morning, when the owner lifts the canvas from the machine, the bystanders scream with horror and no one will ride on the merry-go-round again.

"El niño de los hornos": When a new baby is brought home, no one pays any attention to the little boy who makes mud ovens. One night he lights his toy oven and puts the baby inside.

Most of the stories are roughly divided into two parts, one

of which describes the child in his unique ability to cross the boundary between fantasy and reality. Providing direct contrast with his imaginative adventure is an expressionistically cruel reality which often destroys the child. The impact of the stories thus proceeds directly from a formula by which innocence and fantasy clash at a given moment with the cruelest kind of reality; moreover each episode is presented with carefully controlled understatement, suggesting that the situation presents nothing out of the ordinary.

The artistically apt medium for the fantastic or terrifying events is a prose that can only be classified as poetic. The liberal use of synesthesia and magical incantations underscores the childlike, poetic spontaneity which characterizes the work; certain expressions also recall the form of a child's monotonous chant or a *canción de cuna,* with an insistent cumulative rhythm that gives the impression of a story written for children. Once again the novelist shows her skill in adjusting the language to the subject matter.

Such aesthetic horror, or "naturalismo poético,"[16] contrasts sharply with the highly lyrical and metaphorical prose. This technique, presented in a concentrated form in *Los niños tontos,* is a distillation of the stylized descriptions in *Fiesta al noroeste* and *Pequeño teatro,* and continues in the prose of her later works.

Ana María Matute's second collection of short stories, *El tiempo,* appeared in 1957. Of extremely varied subjects and uneven quality, these stories include themes common to her other works. Each bears the stamp of that combined pessimism and tenderness evident in all her books. Although the language is more selective than that of *En esta tierra,* the reader's attention is often directed to one symbolic object whose presence forms a disturbing leitmotif throughout the story.

"El tiempo," the title story,[17] concerns young Pedro, whose monotonous life is marked by the passing of the train, a symbol of time. He finds his hope for escape in Paulina, and as they leave their village to start a new life, he bends down to help her put on a pair of shoes, which are a symbol of hope and joy. One shoe gets caught as they cross the train tracks, and both are run down by the train.

Although "La ronda" in honor of the boys leaving for the war consists of a night of revelry, Miguel spends his last night in a "ronda hacia dentro," a search for the justification of his existence up to this time. Touched by vague presentiments embodied in an evil-looking lamp which hangs overhead, Miguel leaves the house in pursuit of the answers. Outside, he meets Victor, a schoolmate who had always hated him because of his bullying. When they are alone together, Victor treacherously kills Miguel and leaves for the war, letting everyone believe that Miguel has deserted.

Through a series of lies, the little girl in "Los niños buenos," who wants to go home to her parents, succeeds in creating the impression that her grandfather is a bad influence. After she gives the false idea that she is being undernourished, badly clothed, and encouraged to steal, her father comes and takes her, leaving the old man in utter loneliness.

"Fausto," one of the most chilling stories of the collection, is the name of the cat adopted by a little girl. Her grandfather, an old and feeble organ-grinder, insists that she get rid of the animal, and after failing to make Fausto useful in some way, the little girl kills it by cracking its head on the pavement. The parallel between Fausto and the old man culminates as the child returns home, tells what she has done, and innocently states, "Abuelo, apuesto algo a que te vas a morir muy pronto" (p. 171).

Other stories in this collection also abound in the kind of surprise ending which characterizes the author's later series of short stories. The grotesque element of *Los niños tontos* appears in the combination of innocence and understated horror in "Fausto," in an expanded version of "El corderito pascual" from *Los niños tontos* (now called "El amigo"), and in the strange tales "No hacer nada" and "Mentiras," both stories of an adult's refusal to accept reality.

Several pieces open with a statement around which the author will draw, almost in circular form, the rest of the story. "El tiempo" begins with the train which "Aparecía . . . dando un largo grito, y desaparecía de nuevo tras las rocas agudas" (p. 9). With this reappearing image, a symbol of time, the opening moves from a panorama of the countryside to a picture of the town itself, and then to Pedro, the protagonist. The rest of the story is punctuated by the train whistle, and ends with the departure of the train.

A similarly constructed story begins with the following clinically impersonal statement: "La entrada al mundo de Miguel Bruno costó trescientas sesenta pesetas de honorarios al médico rural, cincuenta más por gastos especiales, tres comidas extraordinarias y la vida de la madre" (p. 73). After a quick summary of Miguel's childhood, the narrative slowly focuses on his house, the rooms in it, and finally the overhead lamp, a prosaic object which Matute turns into a fearful symbol of the unknown.

The interest in the inner man rather than in the external action links this collection closely with *Fiesta al noroeste*, especially in the portrayal of unhappiness and inevitable disillusionment. A preoccupation with the passage of time, which inexorably destroys everything in its path, colors the attitudes of the characters, turns a distorting lens on normal objects, and in general imparts an air of unrest. The style also reflects this tendency, for it is deformed in a way which belies the first impression of realism: the symbolism of objects and a personal interpretation of reality complement the mood of the characters.

The stories concerning children are told from the point of view of a child and include descriptions and reactions which seem appropriately illogical: for example, the child in "El amigo" thinks of his domineering aunt in the following way: "La tía Eulalia era alta, era fuerte, era madrugadora, era trabajadora, era severa, era cumplidora, era exigente, era soltera, era limpia, era sabia, era honrada, era fuerte. La tía Eulalia era horrible" (p. 176).

The melodramatic ending of several of these stories reflects a view of life in which escape from the inevitable anguish of existence is impossible. Thus the protagonists of "El tiempo" are cut down by the very thing from which they are fleeing; in "La ronda," the complex and dramatic relationship of Cain and Abel is reenacted as the weak Victor kills Miguel at the very moment in which a reconciliation would have been possible.

Los hijos muertos, which received the Premio Nacional de Literatura in 1958, is Ana María Matute's most ambitious undertaking to the present day. This novel of over five hundred pages is a panorama of several generations of a family, united by the same blood yet irrevocably separated by different ideas and values. Its length permits a wide scope of ideas, and it expresses the "suma y compendio de toda su producción anterior y en el que cobren su plena intención y sentido cada uno de los problemas vitales, sociales y humanos que había planteado en sus precedentes novelas."[18]

The problems of the divergent generations, personified in the couples Daniel-Verónica and Miguel-Mónica, begin as Isabel, jealous of her cousin Daniel's love for her sister Verónica, has him put out of their home in Hegroz. Daniel establishes himself in Barcelona, sends for Verónica, and later joins the Republicans in the Civil War, in an idealistic commitment to defend "los de abajo." The war over, Daniel returns from a concentration camp and a forced labor mine, a doomed, completely broken and disillusioned man. Verónica and their unborn child have been killed in an air raid. At the insistence of Isabel, Daniel comes back to Hegroz, but only to take a job as forest warden on the estate, and in this way he becomes acquainted with Diego Herrera, the idealistic director of a nearby penal colony.

Unconsciously paralleling the pattern established by Daniel and Verónica, Isabel's adolescent half-sister Mónica escapes to the woods from Isabel's exacting demands and meets secretly with Miguel, a young prisoner in the work colony. When Miguel kills a guard and escapes, Daniel finds him in the mountains, and hides him in his cabin. However, he later changes his mind unexpectedly and forces Miguel to leave. As Daniel shoots down a wolf the next day, he hears another shot, and the wolf and the corpse of Miguel are brought down the mountain at the same time.

This is a bare outline of the plot, for the bulk of the novel acquaints the reader with the past life of most of the characters. Past and present are fused through the technique of flashback: with a word or a sensation, the past comes rushing back to haunt the characters.

Themes which have been developed in former works are all present here: death, the passing of time, the constant repetition of life, the comparison of men with animals, man's inevitable disillusionment. The prose, although relatively straightforward compared with *Los niños tontos* and less bombastic than that of *En esta tierra,* is rich in plastic and sensorial metaphors, lyricism, and symbolism. Frequent adjectival and substantival accumulations create powerful descriptions, which are also pervaded by a bittersweet feeling of compassion on the part of the novelist for her character.

In an excellent review of this book, the critic Antonio Vilanova discusses the universal import of the work: "Lo que confiere una auténtica grandeza a *Los hijos muertos* de Ana

María Matute es justamente que la historia de Daniel Corvo, no es tanto la tragedia humana de su héroe anónimo destrozado por el fracaso y la derrota, como la epopeya colectiva de nuestra guerra civil relatada por un hombre que militó en el bando de los vencidos."[19] Matute's interest in the wider implications of the plot is quite evident and extends beyond the scope of the Republican defeat. The wealth of material, the contrapuntal alternation of past and present, and the panoramic view of several generations are springboards for the psychological drama which forms the true base of the novel. Descriptions of the Civil War are calculated to reinforce the hopeless position of Daniel. The extensive scope of the work permits interpretations of the effects of time, both linear and psychological: its swift passage, the ironic, senseless repetition of events, the realization of the absurdity of life. Daniel's return to Hegroz lays bare the unchanged lives of Isabel and her father, which in turn contrast with the iconoclastic attitudes of the younger generation. The flashback is a device which effectively explores the past, explaining development of character and often providing ironic contrast with the present.

Primera memoria, which won Ana María Matute the coveted Premio Eugenio Nadal, 1959, is the first part of a trilogy entitled *Los mercaderes.* Although the two succeeding novels use some of the same characters, the author has stated that each book has an independent plot structure.

This novel moves from the sweeping view of generations of *Los hijos muertos* to a concentrated focus on the adolescent girl Matia, who lives on an island (Mallorca) with her grandmother, aunt, and cousin Borja. Matia's forbidden friendship with Manuel enrages the cruel and hypocritical Borja, who learns to his dismay that his idol Jorge de Son Major is really Manuel's father. In a burst of rage and jealousy because of Jorge's obvious preference for Manuel, Borja uses the confessional to lie about money he himself stole from his grand-mother; he blames Manuel, who is sent to a reformatory. Matia, out of cowardice, refuses to come forward with the truth.

The main theme of the loss of childhood is framed by a plot designed to heighten this tragic sense of privation. Matute has chosen the fictional autobiography as an apt form for convey-ing Matia's bitterness and the sharp sense of nostalgia for her lost childhood. The presentation is overlayed with a pessi-mism uncommon in a child but prevalent in the author's adult characters. "Qué limpios éramos todavía" (p. 23), a statement made in the beginning of the novel, hints at the tragedy, climaxed by Matia's betrayal by silence, a fitting initiation into the world of adults. Encompassing Matia's own troubled state of mind is the emotion-charged, tense atmos-phere of the family and of the island in general. Cruelty and impassiveness seem inbred in the islanders. The tension of the Civil War is repeated on a minor scale in the war between two groups of boys on the island; and with Borja's envy of Manuel and his revenge, the Cain and Abel theme appears in the plot. The greatest impact of the work comes from another Biblical episode: the betrayal of Christ, unwittingly reenacted by "innocent" children.

The prose of *Primera memoria* is so stylized as to show only Matia's point of view. Descriptions of the grandmother, whom Matia despises, are highly unfavorable: among other epithets, she is called "un dios panzudo y descascarillado" (p. 60), "un enorme y glotón muñecazo" (p. 60), or "Una mole redonda y negra" (p. 76). The prose abounds in colorful sensorial images, and long, flowing, lyrical passages contrast with the violence of fragmentary sentences. Many objects have symbolic value: the sun, the rooster, flowers. The novel-ist also introduces a parenthetical interior monologue. These random thoughts are superimposed on the narration, with the cinematographic effect of a montage of memory-images. Thus, by juxtaposition of past and present, the author effectively recreates her character's shifting point of view: an "objective" narration of adolescence in the form of the *memoria;* random comments and evocations, set off by parentheses, expressed by the adolescent Matia; and finally, the present tense comments of the older Matia, who is writing the story.

For convincing psychological bitterness and for the presentation of an anguished mental climate paralleled by an equally terrible reality, this work is unsurpassed in Matute's production. The prose style combines the most successful elements of her earlier works. What seemed bombastic and baroque to several critics is eliminated here in favor of an extremely poetic prose which is precisely indicative of the peculiar state of mind of the adolescent. Several strange but effective devices add linguistic impact to the novel; in particular, unexpected union of natural elements and people or emotions. Expressions like "Creí que latiría en su voz la misma ira de las flores" (p. 42), and "[flores] de un rojo encendido . . . como el odio cerrado de Lauro" (p. 29) are typical examples. The use of intensely vivid colors in descriptions and a calculated violence in the use of synesthesia ("El sol lucía fuera como un rojo trueno de silencio" [p. 80]) serve as a disturbing, tense background to the solitary drama of Matia.

Because of the careful synthesis of language and idea, the skillful manner in which the uncertainty and unhappiness of the adolescent world is presented, and the poetic description and lyricism, *Primera memoria* must rank, along with *Fiesta al noroeste* and *Los hijos muertos,* as Ana María Matute's best work.

With the publication of *Tres y un sueño* in 1961, the author returns to her own peculiar interpretation of the world of childhood. The "tres" refers to the three child protagonists of the stories; they all participate in "un sueño," that is, an idealized vision of childhood which invariably incorporates fantastic elements, a rejection of the adult world, and an unawareness of reality. Each story treats a different aspect of life, and all include a bitter satire of the world in which the child lives.

"La razón" is what the boy Ivo does not have, for unlike the farmer's family with which he lives, this orphan can see the only three gnomes left in the world. The reason for his special ability, according to the gnome Tano, is that he has moon-drops in his eyes. To convince Ivo that he must continue to believe in fantasy, Tano takes the boy on a tour of the magical world of eternal spring. He is so successful, however, that the boy cannot readjust to reality; to save Ivo's life, Tano is forced to take away his imagination by snatching the moon-drops from his eyes. The gnomes turn to ashes, and Ivo, now completely cured of his "problem," asks the farmer for work and buys himself a pair of long pants.

In "La isla," little Perico wins a magic island at a concession stand in a fair. Attempts to invite family and friends to this island are unsuccessful, for they are too busy with their affairs to listen or are unable to hear him. However, his former nurse, who is in a home for old women who have outlived their usefulness, receives a visit from a bird who announces Perico's approach. When Perico arrives, Aya steps onto the magic island, which "tenía mucha prisa por alejarse de allí" (p. 62).

"La oveja negra" is without doubt the author's strangest literary creation. It concerns a character who lives her whole life in a kind of surrealistic nightmare in which she sees the world through the eyes of a child and believes that she is still a little girl. Her one goal, for which she successively rejects family, religion, and marriage, is the recovery of her lost doll,

Tombuctú, whose symbolic value is clouded and oblique. The ordinarily separate ages of childhood and adulthood are systematically overlapped to provide confusing, often horrifying situations. The story ends as her brothers, speaking of the disgrace she has brought on them, seclude her in the family home, where she is visited by children who daily "kill" her with swords made of lily leaves.

The preoccupation with time evident in other works does not affect the stories in this collection; childhood seems to be a moment suspended in eternity, and it is only after the child returns to "la razón" that the normal linear time begins. This is the reason for the confusion in "La oveja negra": since the protagonist mentally remains a child, time has no meaning for her. She stays at a standstill while others continue growing, and she cannot understand why they do not treat her as a child.

There is an absolute division between childhood and objective reality; one must either remain a child or reject the values of society in order to participate in the imaginative dimension.

Historias de la Artámila, also published in 1961, comprises stories and sketches of the most diverse types, set within the region of Artámila—the thinly disguised Mansilla de la Sierra of the author's childhood. These little works are somber in tone, with none of the colorful prose of her other books, although her tenderness and compassion for the people she describes are still evident. A note of suave melancholy also pervades these stories, for every one concerns some less desirable facet of human nature, the frustration of a dream, or a tragic event. "El mundelo," who is to be imprisoned for knifing a man, stays to help save people instead of escaping from the train wreck on the way to the penitentiary. After serving his term, he is stoned out of town, even though the people are aware of his heroic action. "El río" tells of a little boy who commits suicide because he believes he has killed the schoolmaster by putting in his wine "la flor encarnada de la fiebre dura, la flor amarilla de las llagas y la flor de la dormida eterna" (p. 41). Actually, the man has died of pneumonia. "El pecado de omisión" is committed by a man who takes in an orphaned boy, but instead of schooling him (for he is obviously intelligent) sends him to the mountains as a shepherd. When the boy returns and realizes the difference between himself and his former friends, he murders his "benefactor." These are only representative samples of the twenty-two stories in the volume.

This collection still retains the pessimistic outlook of Matute's other works. Each of the studies contains an inherently tragic situation from which arises a fatalistic conception of life. As Rafael Bosch has noted, it is some element within the story itself—the nature of the protagonists, the insuperable distance between reality and the ideal, the latent cruelty of man—which causes this tragic vision, not a major event such as war: "There is a Chekhovian quality in this beautiful book, an emphasis on the intense lyrical and emotional impact of little things and apparently insignificant happenings."[20]

Of a much more concise, aphoristic nature than *El tiempo*, *Historias de la Artámila* rejects the use of symbolic objects and artistic distortion in favor of a simple, unadorned prose. These pieces are so compact that descriptive paragraphs are at a minimum; the few metaphors used relate directly to nature, perhaps in an attempt to impress upon the reader the intimate relationship of the people of Artámila with the land. Character exposition is not detailed, but through carefully selected traits, the personages become interesting in their own right, transcending the inevitable tragedy which forms part of their existence.

El arrepentido is Matute's fourth collection of short stories, published in 1961. In it she continues many themes noted in previous works: the childhood world of fantasy which encompasses reality ("La luna," in which little Botitas climbs to the moon and disappears on it, or "El embustero," about a little boy who flies with the help of an angel), or the disillusioned adult ("El maestro").

The sentimentality which underlies the author's other works is overemphasized in these stories, notably in "Mañana," in which a disillusioned crook is redeemed by sacrificing himself on Christmas day in a contemporary reenactment of the death of Jesus and the two thieves on the cross. This sentimentality is also noticeable in "El salvamento," in which Timoteo wins his employer's daughter when he bravely tries to save her from drowning although he cannot swim, or in "La señorita Bibiana," whose sudden fainting spells and strange experiences are explained by the young village doctor: "Usted es sonámbula. . . . sabe usted que tiene un gran deseo de ser y hacer felices a los demás" (p. 129).

Social themes, reinforced by use of the Civil War as a background, found in such novels as *Los hijos muertos* or *En esta tierra*, appear again in the two short stories "El hermoso amanecer" and "El maestro." The background of both these narratives is violence and death, but underlying this is the idealism of those who struggle. Although the main protagonists are shot at the end of both stories, a message of hope is apparent, as in the letter to little Remo from his father, who is fighting on the front: " 'Remo, ya sé que te asusta la muerte. Pero nosotros no morimos nunca. . . . Todos los hombres tienen que trabajar en lo que mejor sepan. Yo también he de hacer todavía muchas cosas. Acuérdate de que no hay Muerte. Nosotros no morimos.' Era cierto. Sí: era cierto . . . el Hombre se repetía en el tiempo" (pp. 74–75).

The surprise ending, a recurrent device in Ana María Matute's short stories, appears in this collection. "El arrepentido," for example, leaves his "dirty money" to an orphanage instead of to his nephew; the money which Dionisio ("Los de la tienda") receives from his godfather, and which he in turn secretly gives to a poor friend, turns out to be counterfeit when it is spent at the godfather's grocery store. As in the earlier collections of stories, these surprise endings are not happy; their purpose is to reinforce the tone of pessimism which is evident in even the most fantastic stories.

This collection, however, lacks the interest of Matute's other works. Unrealistic situations, poorly developed characters, and sentimental aspects which seem added as an afterthought do not show Matute's talents to best advantage. The melodramatic element, formerly used with moderation, is abused in this book.

The collection of personal essays *A la mitad del camino*, also published in that most productive year, 1961, is a mixture of nostalgic reminiscences, observations on human nature, and intimate impressions of objects, people, or nature. It is an interesting work because it contains many of the clearest statements of Ana María Matute's attitude toward life, undisguised by fiction.

Belying the words of the title, *Libro de juegos para los niños de los otros* (1961) is not one of Matute's books for children. It is a series of pieces which borrow from the essay, the sketch, and the short story, and use photographs as an integral part of the work. The book is narrated in the first person plural by nameless children who make up "games" which are not games in the ordinary sense, but are fantasy outlets for their repressed envy, hatred, and sense of deprivation. The author's social criticism is apparent in the bitterly accusatory tone of the work, the division between the underprivileged and the privileged, and the obvious empathy with these forgotten children of the poor. The titles of some of these games are meant to shock the reader: "El juego del deseo," "El juego agrio de la envidia," "El juego de los enemigos"; the contents disclose emotions ranging from resignation to bitter hatred. In "El juego del deseo," for example, the children reveal their opinion of a schoolmaster who fawns on the rich: "Tenemos un juego deseado: deseamos coger al embustero, cuando se vuelve a casa, comiéndose las uñas, liando un cigarrillo, con el culo zurcido, a sorberse su sopa de realquilado. Le deseamos muerto, corroido, debajo de las ruedas del coche ese tan grande, azul celeste, que él señala siempre cuando dice:—*Buenas tardes, Doña Consolación.*"

Lurking behind the world of childhood is the knowledge that growing up means a life of hard work in a factory. So the children doggedly act out their games, and at night they play "El juego peligroso," which consists of looking at the sleeping household and thinking about what will happen when they, too, grow up.

Photographs visually reinforce the impact of the text: they portray the "niños de los otros," alone or together, in various attitudes of play. Only in the last picture does an adult appear: a dirty, unshaven old man shuffling along in the background, a ragged child in the foreground. The depressing figures add unsuspected dimensions to the text of the "juego peligroso." The unusual inversion—a picture as commentary to a literary text—gives this collection an original slant.

El río (1963) closely follows the format of *A la mitad del camino,* with its short sketches, observations of life, and so on. In fact, the author has incorporated several pieces from *A la mitad del camino* in this later work. All stories have as a common background the region of Mansilla de la Sierra, to which Ana María Matute returns after it has been submerged by a reservoir. This physical return to the past evokes memories of childhood and comments on the people of the region. Each sketch, tinged with melancholy, is narrated with deliberate understatement, a minor-key tone, and an emphasis on the seemingly unimportant, which recall the sketches of Azorín. Nature, human nature, children, and personal reminiscences are the favored subjects for this work, which also incorporates themes explored in the novels. Time is heavily stressed here —the passage of time, melancholy resignation before inevitable death (be it of humans or animals), children who are children no longer, and a keen sense of nostalgia for things past that cannot return.

Los soldados lloran de noche (1964) is the second novel of the trilogy *Los mercaderes*. Matia does not appear here; the thread of the story begins with Manuel, after his release from the reformatory. Jorge de Son Major has died and recognized Manuel as his son and heir, but Manuel renounces his inheritance in order to make a pilgrimage to learn about Jeza, a fascinating man killed during the Civil War. Manuel finds Jeza's young widow Marta, who recounts her unhappy life before she met Jeza and her "redemption" by him. Together Manuel and Marta offer an obviously futile resistance to the *nacionales;* together they are killed.

The novel uses flashbacks to a great extent, especially in Marta's story of her childhood and adolescence. The obvious religious symbolism of *Primera memoria* is continued in *Los soldados lloran de noche;* Jeza (a Christ-figure) is an ever-present spirit who guides the younger Marta and Manuel. They sacrifice their lives for what he represents. *Los mercaderes*—for whom the trilogy is named—are heirs of the money-changers Christ drove from the temple, who take advantage of their fellows in any possible way and whom Matute has always attacked, though never so vehemently as in this novel.

Algunos muchachos (1968) is Ana María Matute's best collection of short stories to date, once again showing her talent in the short narrative. The pieces treat, in abbreviated form, major themes found in the longer works. The title story blends ideas of lost childhood (symbolized by such images as shipwrecks and beaches) and evil, incarnated in El Galgo, "el hombre que nunca fue muchacho." Juan, the boy-hero of the story, hates El Galgo because he represents a world in which innocence has no place, yet Juan is also fascinated by El Galgo and feels obliged to prove himself by stealing from his family and turning it over to his "friend." After a final robbery, he and El Galgo are to run away together, but the latter actually intends to leave Juan behind. Juan suddenly realizes that the world is divided into victims and profiteers (El Galgo has taken advantage of many others; now he intends to do the same to Juan); he then knowingly sacrifices his life as El Galgo, knife in hand, warns him not to come nearer. He grabs El Galgo in a death grip as the knife enters his body; they both roll into a canal and El Galgo drowns.

A most ordinary event—seeing a photograph of himself and his fiancée—reveals sudden truths to the protagonist of "Muy contento": he realizes that his whole life has been arranged for him by his parents and aunt, and that his future wife will step into their shoes. He feels oppressed by the world the "others" have created for him: the normal, well-ordered side of life, containing neither surprises nor values beyond the material ones. He rebels by burning this world in symbolic form: the factory which he is to inherit.

Claudia (in "No tocar") does not understand the normal values of the world, symbolized by traditions, boyfriends, parents, and so forth. Her main interest is eating enormous amounts of food, although she never gets fat. She views the world in terms of food, even keeping a notebook listing the nutritional value of such diverse things as friends, lightbulbs, and books. She maintains a cold indifference to everything else, including her loving husband, who unwittingly breaks through her aloofness when he points out (approvingly) that Claudia neither laughs nor cries. Suddenly awakened to reality by a seemingly unimportant event, much like the photograph in "Muy contento," she runs away. Her husband finally tracks her to a remote jungle village where she is being worshipped by a tribe of cannibals. He shoots them all, and rushes up to Claudia, only to find that what he thought was his wife is simply a painted stick. He has been searching for the perfection of innocence (Claudia, completely untouched by society, is strangely innocent), which once lost, can never be regained.

"El rey de los zennos" is the most symbol-laden story in the collection. Three parallel incidents take place in different time periods, but have a common setting (a seacoast town) and a unifying character, a young man named Ferbe, the King of the Zennos, people who live in the sea in algae and sponges, waiting for truth and justice to triumph on earth. In the first section, Ferbe preaches this message and the people condemn and burn him; this, with variations, is repeated in the following parts. The story ends as another young man discovers a batch of sponges—a rare find in that place—and picks a great basketful to sell. Suddenly, he feels that "Algo ha desaparecido de la tierra." There are obvious parallels between the hero and Christ: the saviour who preaches peace, his sacrifice, the heedlessness of the people. The awful fact that this incident keeps repeating itself, and probably will continue to do so as long as man remains the same, completely overshadows the resurgence of idealism.

The other stories are equally intriguing. A little girl, in "Cuadernos para cuentas," like so many of Matute's children, displays a frightening combination of innocence and amorality. She is the illegitimate daughter of the cook and the master of the house, and constantly dreams of the day when she and her mother can leave and not be subjected to the abuse of the other children. She hears that her father, a sickly, old man, is going to leave them the bulk of his money, and decides to solve her problems by putting glass splinters in his food. Naturally, the mother is blamed.

"Noticia del joven K" is the latest reworking of the Cain-Abel theme, complete with an epigraph from Genesis ("¿Por qué te has ensañado? ¿Y por qué ha decaído tu semblante?"). "Una estrella en la piel" links the fate of three very diverse beings: a little girl, a chauffeur, and a horse. The girl, whose monologue tells the story, knows that a local caretaker was involved in the deaths of the horse and the chauffeur; she realizes that she, too, will have her turn. After visiting the cemetery for horses, she walks through the woods and sees the caretaker approaching her. The story ends with "De todos modos, sólo a rastras se me llevó."

Although the prose in this collection is relatively simple, certain stylistic trademarks remain very much in evidence; for example, strange adjectival or metaphorical combinations: "El día se vertía como jarabe amarillo" (p. 13); "los hediondos lirios de la orilla, legiones de menudas cabezas mayando de miedo" (p. 29). Much of the work is in the first person, with a tendency toward interior monologue, which transmits the character's viewpoint. Following the pattern established in previous collections, the stories have a thematic and ideological unity; the reader can sense the separation of the individual from society, and the silent, almost unconscious rebellion of the protagonist against injustice.

The trilogy *Los mercaderes* closes with *La trampa* (1969). The locale is the island of *Primera memoria;* the occasion, the grandmother's *falso centenario* (she is celebrating her one-hundredth birthday a year early). Four generations are represented and contrasted through attitude, background, and interaction: the grandmother; Franc (Matia's father), Emilia

(Borja's mother), and Beverly (Matia's mother-in-law); Borja, Matia, Mario, and Isa; and Bear.

Like *Primera memoria*, the novel is introspective; but Matute lays aside the limited focus of a single narrator in favor of a multiple viewpoint, interweaving chapters about the four main characters: Bear, Mario, Isa, and Matia. Each section is autobiographical in tone; present and past stand side by side for scrutiny; people and their motives are dissected in the chilling light of disillusionment. Parenthetical remarks add a third dimension of subconscious thought or commentary superimposed on the text.

After the Civil War, Franc (now a teacher at a midwestern university) sends for Matia; subsequent chapters describe her unsuccessful marriage, her son (Bear), and her divorce. Isa has also had an unhappy experience in love, and is now desperately trying to hold on to Mario, the central character. He touches everyone's life in some way, and his tragic experience serves as the main background to the action. A terrible deed has conditioned his life: as a child, someone tricked him into betraying his father's hiding place, thus causing his death. At the present time, he is the center of an admiring group of youths (which includes Bear) to whom he preaches his philosophy of the destruction of the old myths of society. Mario's lifetime dream of vengeance becomes real when he learns that the man who caused the betrayal is now on the island. He convinces Bear that this man is destroying their group's plans, and together they devise a murder plot: Mario is to hide in the house during the birthday celebration, then escape on Borja's yacht the next morning, the murder and Bear's involvement a *fait accompli* by then.

Matia becomes involved when Mario hides in the abandoned rooms next to hers. They become lovers (their communication born out of doubt, unhappiness, and suffering); he confesses his selfish purpose and resolves not to carry out the plan. Bear, however, has overheard these words and kills the man himself, without trying to hide the crime.

No character realizes his goal; everyone has lost something: a loved one, an ideal, liberty. Each position comes out in the exhaustive self-analysis to which these people submit their acts: the search for self-definition in some; in others, a total hopelessness, a useless rebellion against time, injustice, or unhappiness. An air of fatality pervades the entire work, partially through the past-present technique which colors the events with the foreknowledge of tragedy (although the murder is reserved as a final surprise for the reader), and is constantly emphasized by reference to machines set in motion.

Time returns to play tricks on these characters, and stresses the futility of rebellion: Mario's immurement mirrors his father's experiences; Manuel's gratuitous sacrifice (*Los soldados lloran de noche*) is referred to obliquely, and finally his image and that of Bear merge.

La trampa is a book mainly about adults, all of whom show the symptoms of desolation and resigned unhappiness so prevalent in Matute's other works. The one "hero"—Bear—has committed himself, but the price is self-destruction.

2. The World of Childhood
Una edad total y cerrada

The surprisingly uniform characteristics of the individual children in Ana María Matute's literature correspond to a personal philosophy of life which emerges from her writing, either implied in consistent emphasis on specific qualities of childhood, or, occasionally, stated directly in her essays. She singles out qualities unique to this age: a simplicity which permits the unqualified acceptance of the unusual; an imagination not yet conditioned by society's logic; and innocence. The themes of fantasy and escape, attendant to her interpretation of childhood, derive in part from her dissatisfaction with contemporary values.

A glance at her works reveals an overwhelming predominance of child characters having both major and minor importance. Of interest here are the characters who are most fully developed or most representative of this age: the children in *Los niños tontos, Historias de la Artámila, Fiesta al noroeste, Tres y un sueño,* and *El tiempo. Pequeño teatro* must be included here also: the exact age of Ilé, the protagonist, is never stated (he is probably in early adolescence), but his characteristics so obviously coincide with Matute's ideas of childhood that he too will be considered as a child. This study of Matute's conception of childhood will refer mainly to these books; other works will be mentioned only to emphasize the extent to which an idea is developed.[1]

A fundamental aspect of childhood which separates it from other ages is its static, eternal quality. An acute awareness of time permeates Matute's works; but whereas the older characters' anguish is due in part to their helplessness before the ravages of time, an aura of complete timelessness surrounds the children, giving the impression that this age is an eternal moment, completely dissociated from the normal passage of time. There is a notable lack of references to the passing of days or months. More common are allusions to "días sin mañana, sin tarde ni noche" (*Los niños tontos*, p. 20) or "tiempo detenido" (*Pequeño teatro*, p. 187). Ana María Matute also applies the idea of an unchanging childhood in *Tres y un sueño*. After his trip with the gnome, which, because of the complete omission of any reference to time, seems to last only a few hours, Ivo returns to the world of mortals. Actually, many years have elapsed, but Ivo remains a child: "Algún invierno pasó, con sus veranos y sus épocas templadas. Un día, Ivo regresó por el camino alto. Todos los muchachos habían crecido, y él seguía sin sobrepasar la empalizada del campo amarillo" (p. 41). The girl in "La oveja negra," who continues to believe that she is still a child, does not grow physically either: "La sobrepasaron todos sus hermanos. No crecía" (p. 72). In the story of the "Muchacho crecido," we find the first reference to time only in connection with the boy's growth: "Sin embargo, un día, Dito creció" (*A la mitad . . . , p. 154*).

The lack of references to contemporary events supports the illusion of the extratemporal state of childhood. Throughout the stories dealing with children, there is no attempt to provide an exact topical or historical frame for the action.[2] The few stories that mention specific locations do not use real place names: Oiquixa (*Pequeño teatro*) is the Basque town of Zumaya where Ana María Matute once stayed[3]; Artámila (*Fiesta al noroeste, Historias de la Artámila*) is Mansilla de la Sierra, where the author spent part of her childhood.[4] Even in "La oveja negra," the reader can only assume that the Civil War is a background for part of the girl's story. This unlimited scope of reference also suggests the universal implications of these works: childhood, death, the passage of time go beyond the realm of the author's personal experiences.

The timelessness of the background complements a lack of dynamic movement in both the action and the psychology of the world of childhood. Its boundaries are mental attributes rather than a specific age, for with the loss of particular traits elaborated by the author, one is clearly a child no longer. The evolution of character takes place as the child passes into adolescence; and in those works which cover a long span of years ("El tiempo," for example), the child will lose his infantile qualities as he gains awareness of the world around him.

Childhood seems to be a moment suspended in time, broken only by the change effected when the child becomes an adolescent: "Se encontraban siempre con sorpresa, como se encuentra, al cabo de los años, un amigo de la infancia, alguien que nos dice: '¿Qué fue de todo aquello?' Se ha doblado sin saber cómo la esquina que no parecía definitiva, especial, sino únicamente una esquina más" (*A la mitad* . . . , p. 103).

Those who populate Matute's strange world of childhood form a group apart from "normal" children. The unusual child is the only one capable of entering the realm of illusions; the normal one has already lost his idealism or has never possessed it; he reflects all the qualities of the adults whom he imitates: cruelty, violence, lack of imagination. An emphasis on noisy activity characterizes descriptions of the ordinary youth: "Los chicos son delgados, tienen la piel curtida por el sol. Los chicos venden cosas. Los chicos gritan, tiran piedras, silban, ríen. Los chicos tiene bocas oscuras y pequeñas, tremendas bocas que dicen: '¡Ahí va el gordo!' " ("El amigo," *El tiempo*, p. 177).

The author comments on the significance of childhood

through the eyes of the unusual child, whose ingenuous mind permits him to perceive a world disconnected from ordinary reality. Descriptions of these special youths offer striking similarities: deliberately homogeneous qualities and common experiences point to a generalization of childhood in which the individual (although often interesting in his own right) forms part of a collective picture. Many of these children are nameless, especially in the short stories, and are designated with a generic term: "La niña tenía la cara oscura" (*Los niños tontos*, p. 9); "Aquel niño era un niño distinto" (*Los niños tontos*, p. 33). The girl in "La oveja negra" is called *hija*, *hermana*, and so forth.

The physical appearance of the young characters also differentiates them from other children. One is extremely fat; some are thin or quite ugly. Another is paralyzed, and Juan Medinao, of *Fiesta al noroeste*, has an oversized head. The child's eyes, however, have a radiance which minimizes his unattractiveness. The emphasis placed on this feature also groups these children in a special class: "[Ilé] estaba siempre muy sucio, con escamas relucientes pegadas a la piel y a la ropa. Pero tenía los ojos azules, como mar que duerme" (*Pequeño teatro*, p. 10). Blue eyes, golden eyes, or eyes that shine brightly distinguish such a child; they are a symbol of his special status and separate him from others: "No olvidaré nunca la transparencia hueca fija en sus ojos de color de miel" ("Bernardino," *Historias* . . . , p. 96); "Y vi sus ojos de pupilas redondas, que no eran negras sino de un pálido color de topacio, transparentes, donde el sol se metía y se volvía de oro" ("Los chicos," *Historias* . . . , p. 62). "La razón" provides an explanation for these shining eyes: Tano tells the other gnomes that they live only because the boy Ivo has moon-drops in his eyes (*Tres y un sueño*, p. 28). These moon-drops, perhaps a reflection of the light which heralds the world of fantasy, symbolize the imaginative capacities of

ANA MARÍA MATUTE

the special child. The author uses the blue, gold, or shining
eyes of the special child to indicate that he possesses the two
most essential attributes of childhood: imagination and innocence.

These two vital qualities are inseparable: innocence—the
absence of contamination by dull or cruel reality—allows the
extraordinary child to give full play to his imagination; once
reality has shown him the impossibility of his dream world, he
ceases to be a child. Marco exalts the uncorrupted soul of Ilé
when he describes him as "la vida pura" (*Pequeño teatro*, p.
182); this statement (that untrammelled imagination is what
is *real* and that the symbolic child who lives it is "pure" life in
the two senses of *unadulterated* and *authentic*) is the most
clear-cut expression of the underlying quality of these children. Ana María Matute also supplies the key to the character
of childhood in a portrait of the same boy: "Ilé Eroriak era de
cortos alcances, tardo en hablar, y había quien hallaba es-
túpida su sonrisa. Sus escasas palabras a menudo resultaban
incoherentes y poca gente se molestaba en comprender lo que
decía. Sin embargo, había un rayo de luz, fuerte y hermosa
luz, que atravesaba el enramado de sus confusos pensamientos
y le hería dulcemente el corazón. Su grande, su extraordinaria
imaginación le salvaba milagrosamente de la vida. También
su ignorancia y, sobre todo, aquella fe envidiable y maravi-
llosa" (*Pequeño teatro*, p. 11).

The unique physical and mental characteristics of the special child segregate him from others in a loneliness heightened by the indifference or hostility of both adults and peers.
The keen awareness of one's solitude, which evolves into a
more conscious estrangement in adolescence and adulthood,
crystallizes in Matute's treatment of these children: "Muchas
veces me he dicho que el niño está siempre solo, que es quizás
el ser más solo de la creación" (*A la mitad . . .* , p. 133).
Even the briefest survey of this writer's works reveals the

remarkable number of lonely children: *Pequeño teatro,* "El tiempo," "La ronda," "Fausto," "El amigo," "Chimenea," *Fiesta al noroeste,* "El incendio," "Pecado de omisión," "Caminos," "La fiesta," "Bernardino," "Los pájaros," and "La razón" include children who are orphaned; others are separated from their parents ("Los niños buenos," "La isla"). Their ostracism by other children intensifies their desolation: Juan Medinao is poignantly aware of his loneliness, even at the age of five (*Fiesta al noroeste,* p. 44); a little girl of *Los niños tontos* is completely ignored by her playmates (p. 9).

Most people are incapable of understanding the child's chimerical world. A woman who sees the collection of "stars" that the little girl in "Fausto" has pasted on the wall, dismisses them as trash (*El tiempo,* p. 156); the brothers in "El perro perdido" mistake the dog's howl for the sound of the wind (*Historias . . . ,* p. 168). These young protagonists sense their separateness and do not expect others to understand them; inversely, they cannot grasp the sentiments and motivations of others: "¿Cómo explicar que las cosas que él sabía, pensaba y veía, tampoco las comprendían los demás? ¡Cuánto trabajo le hubiera costado hacerse entender, para que al final tampoco le creyeran!" ("La razón," *Tres y un sueño,* p. 10).

One of the essays in *A la mitad del camino* elaborates on the reasons for the child's solitude, in a description of the schism between children and adults: "Un niño es otra cosa, que un hombre o una mujer que aún no ha crecido. Como si tuviera un cuerpo distinto, más que un cuerpo pequeño. Su mundo interior apenas tiene puntos de contacto con el mundo interior del hombre o de la mujer que será. La infancia es una edad total, una vida cerrada y entera. . . . Los mayores, para los niños, no sólo somos más altos, somos distintos. Nuestras razones nunca pueden ser las suyas" (p. 133). The author's idea that the child is so completely separated from older people that he lives on a different plane adds another basic concept to her original philosophy: the isolated nature which causes his solitude will also encourage him to create his own world through his unique qualities. "¿Los niños que no mueren, dónde andarán?" is a question frequently posed in Matute's works.[5] This further comment on "la vida cerrada y entera" shows that adolescence is not a simple continuation of childhood; once an experience shatters the child's fragile world, he loses his ability to shut out reality and joins the other adults in their unhappy search for the "child who has not died." Attitude rather than age divides childhood from the other periods of life. Once childhood ends and his childlike qualities disappear, the character must begin a new life, completely cut off from his former existence: "Al dejar la infancia se sobrenace más que se continúa" (*A la mitad . . .* , p. 133). Matute intimates this idea in other books, notably *Primera memoria,* when the protagonist cries out, "¿Será verdad que de niños vivimos la vida entera, de un sorbo, para repetirnos después estúpidamente, ciegamente, sin sentido alguno?" (p. 20).

The attributes of the special child also motivate his reaction to the world in which he lives. His special characteristics, heightened by the awareness of his solitude and the indifference of others, prepare the child to reject reality and fabricate a hermetic existence which excludes all others. Thus the theme of escape appears as one of the basic foundations of Ana María Matute's literature. A pattern of disillusionment-escape determines much of the older characters' reaction to life; increased contact with social or ideological wrongs makes withdrawal from the world a major preoccupation.[6] The need for escape takes shape early, but unlike the adult, the child's escape is generally spontaneous, resulting from an imaginative state coupled with a growing awareness of his solitude. Such escape may be actual physical movement or a more subtle withdrawal involving the imagination.

Physical escape usually takes place in a flight to nature, which is more receptive than the human world. Ilé of *Pequeño teatro* finds comfort in his solitary visits to the sea, which he considers his true home (p. 46). Ivo prefers nature to the company of people who do not understand him ("La razón," *Tres y un sueño*, p. 10); the little girl in "La oveja negra" runs to the woods from the stifling atmosphere of her house. Nature is the only friend of "La niña fea," for there no one tells her to go away (*Los niños tontos*, p. 9).

An unrestricted world becomes temporarily accessible through a special group of people who form an intermediate step between physical and mental escape. The travelling actors, puppeteers, acrobats, and so forth who appear in many works, offer a way of forgetting everyday life and temporarily entering a realm unlimited by reality.[7] According to the author, their function transcends mere entertainment: "Pienso en ellos [los cómicos], repito, y me digo si su verdadera misión no será esa: la extraña misión errante de llevar el sueño o la esperanza, o de llamar a la conciencia de los hombres, en un mundo sin techo y sin paredes" ("Siempre los cómicos," *A la mitad* . . . , p. 46). The bright light, ever-present in the world of imagination and perhaps the surest sign of its presence, surrounds the *cómicos* and their carts: "Había luz dentro del carro, luz de velas, como en un palacio de juguete o de cuento" (*Fiesta al noroeste*, p. 88). "Aparecieron los dos carros. Sus ruedas se reflejaban con un brillo último, claro y extraño, en las aguas del río" ("El incendio," *Historias* . . . , p. 9). These travelling players offer a veil for reality to people of all ages. With their tempting prospect of both mental and physical escape, they also attract the unhappy children. "La oveja negra" leaves home and joins a travelling puppeteer; Dingo and Juan associate their projected flight from Artámila with the travelling players (*Fiesta al noroeste*, pp. 84–85). This type of escape, however, is only a first step; the indispensable quality of the special world described by the author is still imagination.

Ana María Matute makes it clear that imagination is a necessary factor in life; it alone can temper man's unhappiness. "No quiero referirme aquí a esos inevitables embustes de que todos vivimos, sino a esa grande y hermosa mentira que es tal vez la única forma de vida posible. ¿Quién desea realmente la verdad? Solamente los santos o los demonios. Los hombres, las mujeres, los muchachos, buscamos ese brillo o ese velo, que también puede llamarse esperanza. La realidad no siempre encaja con el deseo" ("Mentiras," *A la mitad* . . . , pp. 109–10). Fancy permits the special child to accept a plane of life detached from everyday existence; his innocence and imaginative powers save him from his unhappiness and solitude. For this reason the writer implies that childhood, spared the disillusionment which plagues the older characters, and within reach of a magic world, is the most desirable time of all, "una edad hermosa, una edad en que el color de la hierba era distinto, y la campana del puerto sonaba alegre, en vez de triste, cuando los buques partían" (*Pequeño teatro*, p. 97).

Since his reactions are unconditioned by experience, the child can spontaneously accept the dual planes of fantasy and reality. Thus Ivo is not in the least surprised to see a gnome, but simply tries to catch him; Perico, having hit the bull's-eye three times, considers it quite proper to win a magic island; and the girl in "La oveja negra," wandering through the surrealistic nightmare of her whole life, never stops to question.

The few adults who retain childlike attributes consciously evade reality to participate in these imaginative excursions. Marco, with his "ojos de los locos, de los niños . . . los ojos del sueño, de lo que no existe" (*Pequeño teatro*, p. 110), affirms his desire to enter this unique place in his statement that he could never live without dreams (p. 84). However, most adults are too involved with materialistic preoccupations to be aware of this second plane, or are so lacking in imagination that involvement is impossible. Perico's invitations to visit his magic island go unheeded: "Fui navegando por todas las costas y quise invitar a mucha gente . . . pero ellos no me conocían ya. . . . Luego, llamé a los pilletes, y tampoco me comprendieron. . . . Fui a por ellos [mis padres] pero estaban de viaje" ("La isla," *Tres y un sueño,* pp. 61–62).

An inversion of traditional standards is evident in the child's unhesitating acceptance of the fantastic, while conversely judging ordinary aspects of life to be unusual or malevolent. This Matute artistically conveys through the poetization of reality, and through a mental process by which the child rejects the world by dehumanizing people, and accepts the fantastic by the inverse process of humanizing animals and objects. This process is most striking in *Pequeño teatro,* with the extensive treatment of the theme of "all the world's a stage." Through the eyes of both Ilé and Ana María Matute, the people of Oiquixa are reduced to the size of the marionettes in the town's puppet show. The stranger Marco reminds Ilé of a puppet (p. 43), and the waiters in Kepa's hotel are marionettes who spring to life when the owner manipulates their strings (p. 53). In *Fiesta al noroeste,* the unhappy Juan Medinao compares Salomé to an exotic insect (p. 38). By dehumanization, adults forfeit their normal status and become strange beings in a world that the child neither understands nor accepts. This attitude also implies a dissociation from society. The reduction in size of the adults minimizes their importance in the eyes of the child, who in this way symbolically refuses the imposition of their own reality and standards on him.

Human attributes are also applied to animals: not only do these creatures react as sensitive human beings, but several are subject to the same cruelty and violence that dominate

45

their masters. Cats seem to have assimilated human emotions, such as hatred ("La razón," *Tres y un sueño*, p. 27) or envy ("El negrito de los ojos azules," *Los niños tontos*, p. 15), and often rebel against the child, for example, the cat who tears out a boy's symbolic blue eyes in *Los niños tontos*. Matute provides a clear equation between cats and humans in "Fausto" (see p. 17 above). Other animals more intimately parallel the world of childhood itself. The "Corderito pascual," a gift of a moneylender to his friendless son, is sacrificed by the father on Easter, thus depriving the lonely boy of his only friend. Birds, dogs, and butterflies appear most frequently in works dealing with children. References to birds, flight, wings, and so forth, suggest or accompany the theme of escape[8]; dogs are closest to the children and often echo their sentiments: "El perro, tendido a sus pies toda la noche, derramó dos lágrimas" ("El negrito de los ojos azules," *Los niños tontos*, p. 17).

The process of humanization extends to inanimate objects. Ilé imagines that the waves of the sea harbor "pequeños seres, pobres seres pintados, pobres cuerpos de mentira" (*Pequeño teatro*, p. 24), and just as most of the townspeople have doll-like attributes, the real marionettes assume human proportions (p. 99). In other stories the imagery is no less imaginative: a wooden table thirstily sucks up spilled wine ("Los alambradores," *Historias de la Artámila*, p. 45); a pair of tongs abandoned on the hearth seems like a large, black animal ("La razón," *Tres y un sueño*, p. 24). Even immaterialities such as shadows or words assume animate properties: "Pero su sombra temblaba en el agua, tremenda, negra, humana" ("El tiempo," *El tiempo*, p. 11). "No comprendía por qué continuamente las palabras de sus padres estaban dando vueltas y vueltas en torno a aquellas cuatro paredes blancas, como abrazándolas" ("El tiempo," *El tiempo*, p. 12).

Another element of the child's *mundo interior* is a pure,

dazzling light, which imparts an aura of the unreal. It often emanates from gold-colored objects and recalls the presence of light in the eyes of the child. The island that Perico wins is of gold ("La isla," *Tres y un sueño,* p. 57); a boy describes an imaginary tree as of a gold so bright that it hurts his eyes ("El árbol de oro," *Historias* . . . , p. 155); a child will know of the arrival of the Three Kings when the whole room turns to gold ("El rey," *Historias* . . . , p. 113). This special light may also be present within the person concerned, connected with some form of happiness or self-realization: "En algún lugar del alma de Ilé, empezó a crecer una luz. Una luz punzante y hermosa, que tal vez era la felicidad" (*Pequeño teatro,* p. 226). The land of Eternal Spring that Ivo visits also contains the golden light: "Por los cementerios de flores y de mariposas, en espera de la primavera: por los cementerios *luminosos* de las *luciérnagas* y los escondidos jardines de *girasoles,* por los valles subterráneos donde duermen los niños que no han muerto, tendidos, con los ojos abiertos y las manos llenas de arena de *oro*" ("La razón," *Tres y un sueño,* pp. 39–40; italics added).

Matute reinforces the psychology of the child with a style adjusted to show his reactions to life. Style and idea are inseparable in these works, each contributing to the total vision which makes her literature unique. Outstanding is her stylistic interpretation of the child's view of his world, in which reality and fantasy intermingle until the boundaries are not clearly distinguishable. According to the author, the child possesses a keen sensorial awareness and perceives with equal precision qualities of both subjective and objective reality through his senses and his imagination.[9] To illustrate this, she reduces abstractions (which would presumably be difficult for the child to comprehend) to concrete entities, with a charming balance between traditional—even sentimental—symbols and strikingly original ones. A good example is "La razón," in

47

which Tano, the gnome, shows Ivo the sleeping household. A style reminiscent of a story for children accompanies the poetic translation of abstract concepts (such as miserliness, love, fear) into their symbolic material counterparts. The miserly couple who keep Ivo are asleep: "Por el techo vagaban sus sueños: sucias monedas, billetes de banco, doblones de oro. También había un metal duro, golpeado, sujeto por una cuerda.—Es el corazón—dijo el gnomo" (*Tres y un sueño*, p. 33). However, the woman's one gratuitous feeling is her love for her son, and among the dreams of money shines "una lucecilla, como una mariposa, dándose golpes contra las paredes" (p. 33). In another room the swineherd trembles in his sleep; over his head hovers a black bird, which symbolizes fear (p. 34). Tano and Ivo next visit the school and see stones and mud coming from the mouths of the children; the one special child has a golden butterfly on his forehead (p. 38).

A materialization of emotions also illustrates the child's thoughts. A tickling fear is like being "rodeados de mariposas negras, de viento, de las luces verdes que huían sobre la tierra grasienta del cementerio" ("Don Payasito," *Historias* . . . , p. 16); intense happiness is like the sun illuminating a glass of wine ("El tiempo," *El tiempo*, p. 14); a shiver of fear is like a snake ("Don Payasito," *Historias* . . . , p. 19); envy becomes a scratching animal ("Envidia," *Historias* . . . , p. 151); and death is announced by falling leaves ("El perro perdido," *Historias* . . . , p. 167). Matute also remembers her own childhood counterparts of certain emotions: "El lobo era el miedo, el sapo la crueldad gratuita, la revancha injustificada" ("La selva," *A la mitad* . . . , p. 9).

Poetic conversion is not limited to abstractions; commonplace objects also undergo a metamorphosis which makes them disproportionate with reality by magnifying their significance. A tiny window becomes a thirsty mouth, a watchful eye, or a shameful wound (*Pequeño teatro*, pp. 199–200); a road stretches out like a fan of fantastic cards ("Los niños buenos," *El tiempo*, p. 128); humid spots on the wall take the shape of strange maps ("Los niños buenos," *El tiempo*, p. 130); broken bottles and tin cans are fallen stars ("Fausto," *El tiempo*, p. 155); and a shining layer of dust on a stone patio recalls "al que impregna las alas de las mariposas" (*Fiesta al noroeste*, p. 37).

The imaginative world of childhood is always balanced with objective reality. Even within the most fantastic sketches of *Los niños tontos*, reality is contiguous with the dream-world, for aesthetic as well as ideological reasons. To illustrate the polarity of the child's world and the real world, there is contrast of character or situation. The farmer's family, miserly and materialistic, are foils for the imaginative Ivo and his gnome; instead of a golden tree which entrances one boy, only barren land appears to another ("El árbol de oro," *Historias . . .* , p. 157); the "fallen stars" which the child in "Fausto" gathers are in reality broken glass. Modifying the poetic prose which usually describes this age, Ana María Matute may employ contrast in the form of a simple understatement to show the divergence between the two worlds. The "impartial" treatment of this opposition provides an irony which underscores the crucial effect of such differences.

"La oveja negra," from *Tres y un sueño*, illustrates many of Matute's theories of childhood: this presentation of life as an absurd nightmare explores the implicit incongruity between reality and dreams; symbolism and stylistic devices enhancing the child's point of view provide a background for a lifetime, for "La oveja negra" lives her whole life believing she is still a little girl. The author masterfully wields the strange dualism caused by the intermingling of reality and fantasy. The girl escapes from home as a child, goes through the Civil War, marries, sees her husband killed, has a child, and returns home again. Only in the last few pages does one realize that

these nightmarish events are the story of her life; to complete
the circle, the girl is brought back to the very house from
which she escaped as a child. Throughout her life, the protagonist, who characteristically remains nameless, views everything with a child's mind and often accepts situations without
complete understanding. The story is divided into seven sections, each containing some major event in her life. The first,
"El bosque," describes her childhood, her disaffection from
the family, and the solace she finds only in nature. A child's
shoe, cast in silver, symbolizes life within the house: "Odiaba
aquel zapato, en la horrible vitrina de la sala grande" (p. 66).
Even as a child, she is marked by the fatality which will
continue throughout her life: "Ésta traerá desgracia a quien la
quiera, es de las que llevan el mal allí donde pisan" (p. 67).
The loss of her doll Tombuctú, who represents her childhood,
marks a turning point in her existence. She devotes her life to
the search for the doll, and the hope of finding it provides the
motivation for her actions.

In the second section, "Dos muchachos negros," the beginning of her adolescence and the incipient rebellion characteristic of this stage of life assume symbolic form. Two Negro
boys with swords made of lily leaves offer to help find Tombuctú and they run away together. The grandmother provides the first clue that the girl has started to grow up, as she
yells, "¿No ves que ya no eres una niña?" (p. 79). She tempts
her granddaughter to stay by holding out the silver shoe. In
desperation, the girl throws a penknife at her and recovers it
smeared with blood. Her brothers explain this incident later as
they state, "mató a disgustos a la abuela" (p. 131).

She next joins a hunchback who owns a travelling marionette show ("El hombre"). Following a pattern set by other
characters, the girl sees the opportunity for escape in the
travelling players; in this case, such escape is twofold: physical isolation through running away and a psychological aliena-

tion as she retreats into the security of childhood through her imagination. This she does willingly, but is frustrated in her search for Tombuctú, when she finds that her doll is not among the marionettes.

In her wanderings she encounters a pilgrimage, but she rejects religion as she sees that what she thought was her doll is "una crucecilla de palo, mal clavada, muerta" (p. 92). "Las mujeres" comprises the beginning of the Civil War.[10] In a camp she searches for Tombuctú and thinks she sees him hanging around the neck of a soldier, but is again disillusioned (p. 101). They go away together and he is killed.

"El niño" is a small boy who appears next to the protagonist and calls her "mother." They visit a church, only to see a mob burn it and kill the clergy. Suddenly the child is grown and leaves on a train. After other odd adventures ("El organillero"), she returns home; her brothers put her in the old house, where she tells the children who come to stare at her that she too is a child ("La tristeza"). The story closes with one of those strange endings so typical of Matute's works concerning children: "Los niños se lanzaron sobre ella con las espadas en alto. Pero sus espadas estaban hechas de hojas de lirio, y se doblaban sobre su pecho. No podían atravesar su corazón, y de este modo el juego duraría mientras no crecieran, y podrían venir todos los días a matarla" (p. 137).

"La oveja negra" is a study of inability to cope with reality and the wish to evade unacceptable situations. The reappearing image of Tombuctú incarnates the yearning to re-create the happiest moments of childhood, yet each new discovery of the doll only brings disappointment. Thus the heroine symbolically rejects other alternatives (religion, marriage, children) as false substitutes in her desperate attempt to retain her childhood.

The author neatly separates each period of this girl's life by references to water: when she runs away for the first time, she and the two boys go to the river; before seeing the hunchback, she wades into the river up to her waist (p. 82). She meets the religious procession on the seashore, and after they leave, the tide rises and the waves reach her (p. 92). The soldier is shot when they are near a river; she climbs into a boat and wakes up to discover her son (p. 105). When she finally returns home, she must cross the river to get to the old house (p. 133). Matute has chosen this symbol to suggest the passage of time, obscuring specific lapses of time so that objective reality (the comments of others that the girl has grown up) and subjective reality (the girl's belief that she has not aged) are purposely confused.[11]

The contrast found within the character of the "black sheep" herself (a grown woman with a child's mentality) is repeated in other works: the more striking examples include the introduction of grotesque elements that clash with the poetic description of the child's personality and world. The child may become an innocent monster who unwittingly commits horrible acts as if they were perfectly natural. Matute inserts incongruous details with a studied simplicity, stylistically minimizing the impact of fantasy and reality, for it is generally some effect of reality that leads the child to act in this way. The little girl in "Fausto," who previously collected "stars" from the ground, kills her pet cat because her grandfather insists that she get rid of it. After failing to get Fausto a new home, "La niña cogió a *Fausto* por las patas de atrás y le golpeó la cabeza contra el bordillo de la acera. *Fausto* tosió por última vez. Y ésta, sí que parecía un hombre. Lo dejó cuidadosamente tendido en el charquito rojo, que, poco a poco, se agrandaba bajo su cabeza rota. Los ojos de Fausto se apagaron" (*El tiempo,* p. 170). The horror is even greater as she compares the cat with her grandfather and states that he, too, will die soon (p. 171). *Los niños tontos* abounds in the bizarre element: "El niño que no sabía jugar" indulges in pinching off little animals' heads with his dirty fingernails; another boy, puzzled at the attention paid to his new baby brother, puts the child into his toy oven and lights it. The use of the grotesque for a surprise ending, presented in an understatement, is a constant device in this book.

The boundaries between reality and fantasy first blur, then suddenly fracture in *Los niños tontos*. Juan Luis Alborg has noted the divergence of the two antithetical worlds in his definition of the title of the book: "Choques de soñadores mentalidades infantiles contra las trágicas realidades cotidianas que rompen . . . la fantasía de sus ilusiones quiméricas . . . en soñarlas . . . reside su imposible, su delicada 'tontería.' "[12] The *choques* he mentions are of interest here. In almost every story in *Los niños tontos*, the child longs for the fulfillment of a dream: washing herself with the moon ("Polvo de carbón"), finding out what the sea is like ("Mar"), riding on a merry-go-round that is closed down ("El tíovivo"), or hunting "todas las estrellas de la noche, las alondras blancas, las liebres azules, las palomas verdes, las hojas doradas y el viento puntiagudo" ("El niño del cazador," p. 43). Significantly, one of the rare times when the writer openly states that the child is happy is when he gets his wish and participates in his fantastic world. During this moment of plenitude, however, the author abruptly interpolates the world of reality. The consequences are irreparable: hardly a child is able to survive the experience and still retain his innocent state.

The meeting of fantasy and reality usually results in the death of the child, for there does not seem to be a manner of coexistence of these two worlds. In at least eleven cases, the child dies when he is forced back to adult reality or achieves his greatest moment of imaginative power. The theme of death is apparent throughout Ana María Matute's works, although the interpretation varies according to the age of the character. In childhood, it reinforces the idea that this fragile

world is easily broken by contact with reality, and symbolically, that the child is not father of the man.[13]

Historias de la Artámila includes several children who die
after an encounter with a world they do not understand. A
little boy who feels responsible for the death of a schoolmaster
he hates, kills himself because he believes too strongly in his
imaginative world: "Le maté yo a don Germán, le mezclé en
el vino la flor encarnada de la fiebre dura, la flor amarilla de
las llagas y la flor de la dormida eterna. Adiós, padre, que
tengo remordimiento. Me perdone Dios, que soy el asesino"
("El río," p. 41).

Los niños tontos abounds in stories ending with the death
of a child. Matute usually prefers to circumvent the actual
word *muerte* and insinuates the child's death through her
own allusions or the cries of the protagonists. As in the case of
"Fausto," the author chooses to describe death so evasively in
order to maintain the poetic level of the story while introduc-
ing the realistic elements essential to the contrast she wishes to
establish. The comparison of such a horrible reality with the
poetic and fantastic atmosphere that permeates *Los niños
tontos* is sufficient to provide the necessary degree of horror.
The death of the "niña fea" is simply marked by these words:
"Un día, la tierra le dijo: 'Tú tienes mi color.' A la niña le
pusieron flores de espino en la cabeza, flores de trapo y de
papel rizado en la boca, cintas azules y moradas en las muñe-
cas" (p. 9). The story of the child who wants to wash herself
with the moon ends in a similar fashion: "Estrechamente
abrazada a la luna, la madrugada vió a la niña en el fondo de
la tina" ("Polvo de carbón," p. 12); and the author implies a
horrible death in the story of the boy who takes a ride on the
merry-go-round that is not working: "Cuando el sol secó la
tierra mojada, y el hombre levantó la lona, todo el mundo
huyó, gritando. Y ningún niño quiso volver a montar en aquel
tíovivo" ("El tíovivo," p. 37).

The most direct expression of the death of a child because of his inability or refusal to cope with the adult world is found in the essay "Los muchachos crecidos." After describing the period which immediately follows childhood as a "zona triste," Matute continues: "Pero me acuerdo de Dito porque no la superó. Dito murió en seguida, imprevistamente. . . . Sé que Dito era demasiado niño, demasiado pequeño, demasiado imbuido de aquella grande y perdida primavera, y no lo pudo soportar" (*A la mitad* . . . , p. 155). This is simply a resumé of the author's fictional works. The "grande y perdida primavera" is undoubtedly the best and happiest time of life; the loss of childhood is something so terrible that few are able to survive it.

Ana María Matute's personal vision of life dictates the norms for her literary world, and nowhere is she so subjective as in her treatment of childhood. Her interest in children, her disregard of objective analysis, the tenderness and pity evident in her treatment of them, are a far cry from the objective approach to literature so popular today. Such subjectivity may stem from personal experience: Ana María Matute has always stressed the importance of her own childhood. She has doubtless transferred much of her own childhood to her literature, for a suggestively autobiographical note permeates her writing.[14] Her picture of childhood reflects a personal and unique conception of life. The children follow a specific pattern: they are solitary, misunderstood creatures lost in a hostile world of adults. Innocence and imagination help them to escape reality into a partially or totally fantastic world. The author's obviously pessimistic outlook, however, does not permit the child to remain in this state: the inevitable intrusion of reality destroys his world. Childhood must end, with death or with maturity. The loss of childhood is irrevocable; the character must begin life anew, completely cut off from his former state.

Thus the ending of childhood forms the foundation of a fatalistic outlook. The loss of the child "que no murió ni está en ninguna parte" will be mourned by the older characters, whose wretched existence is made more wretched still by nostalgic remembrances of their own childhood, for the slow process of disillusionment has erased from their souls the imagination and innocence of a lost paradise.

3. The World of Adolescence
El tiempo de esperanza

Ana María Matute apparently believes that young characters can best reveal the insights which she is attempting to convey to the reader; she is fascinated by childhood and adolescence —the formative stages of life—and the results of innocence or idealism pitted against the forces of reality. Her adolescent characters show this pattern most clearly: Valba and her brothers (*Los Abel*), Cristián and Soledad (*En esta tierra*), several characters in *El tiempo* (Pedro and Paulina of "El tiempo," Miguel Bruno of "La ronda," Martín Dusco of "No hacer nada," and Babel of "La frontera del pan"), Matia and Borja of *Primera memoria*, Zazu (*Pequeño teatro*), Manuel (*Los soldados lloran de noche*), Bear (*La trampa*), and the adolescent Isabel, Daniel, Verónica, Miguel, and Mónica (*Los hijos muertos*). To these must be added a host of secondary characters who reinforce the total picture of this period.

Although, as in Matute's vision of childhood, the idea that psychological, not chronological, age determines "growth," and that the boundaries of adolescence conform to a timetable of the author's creating, her treatment of the adolescent greatly differs from that of the child. Discarding the self-contained, static qualities of childhood, she concentrates on the adolescent's personality evolution, its dynamism and development through contact with others, through an awareness of self and surroundings, and through the resolution of conflicts which generally arise from interior problems: adjustment, self-realization, a dilemma of ideals, desires, and reality, and eventual disillusionment.

The character's initiation into adolescence begins with the truncation of childhood, a result of the loss of innocence, a sharp clash with reality, a knowledge of death, or involvement in a situation which the ingenuous child cannot accept. This abrupt change marks the radical separation between these two periods of life, and provides the ending in several stories. One of these occurs in "La razón" (*Tres y un sueño*): Ivo's inability to adjust to reality after his trip to the magic land forces the gnome to remove the symbolic moon-drops from his eyes: "Ivo se levantó y sacudió el polvo de su traje. Cuando llegó a la alquería . . . dijo:—Dame trabajo.—Al día siguiente pidió que le cortaran el pelo, y luego se fue a Lucas:—Ya soy mayor tengo ya la razón. . . . Le dio la llave del baúl. Ivo buscó el dinero, y fue a comprarse un pantalón largo" (pp. 44–45). A child in *Los niños tontos* suddenly matures after having to accept the death of a friend; he sheds the characteristics of childhood as he, too, receives the obvious status symbol of his growth: a man's suit of clothes ("El niño al que se le murió el amigo," p. 49). The death of his father precipitates Pedro into a lonely life which prematurely ages and hardens him ("El tiempo," p. 22). The little girl of "Los niños buenos" loses her childhood when she begins her career of lies (*El tiempo*, p. 134); Juan Medinao grows suddenly after he plans to rob money from his father (*Fiesta al noroeste*, p. 84). In the terse prose used to mark this moment, the author pinpoints the transition for Valba Abel: "Ninguna estrella. Mejor. El frío me lamía la piel, daba diente con diente, y la llama del farol agonizando daba un compás inseguro a las sombras. Y de pronto, sentí que la infancia quedaba lejos, que se borraba y se perdía irremisiblemente" (*Los Abel*, p. 48). Ana María Matute has also commented on the abruptness of this change: "A aquella edad nuestra bastaba a veces sólo un día para crecer bárbara, monstruosamente" (*El tiempo*, p. 248).

Although the adolescents' common experiences and fate

lend themselves to generalizations about this period, the emphasis on personal development also individualizes each character. Matute prefers psychological characteristics to physical description, which she compresses into a few sketchy details. Typical of this deemphasis of pictorial description and highlighting of a distinctive spiritual trait is the characterization of Zazu in *Pequeño teatro*. Recurrent phrases recall her "manos de ladrón," "ojos de distinto color," "pelo lacio"; her insatiable desire for love, however, receives more attention: "Zazu iba a rastras del amor, con su gran sed, con sus pies descalzos y sus manos vacías. Zazu pensaba siempre en el amor, y nunca había amado a nadie. El cuerpo de Zazu era un cuerpo duro y bello, un cuerpo delgado y casi adolescente. . . . Zazu tenía un cuerpo apretado y sencillo, un cuerpo ahogadamente ceñido a sus caminos de sangre, como largos ríos de sed. Zazu tenía un pequeño cuerpo amargo y triste, que la empujaba dulcemente, . . . fatalmente. . . . Ella amaba su cuerpo y sentía piedad por él, como se apiada uno de los perros perdidos que gimen en las cunetas, como se siente piedad por los gritos de los niños que sueñan en naufragios" (pp. 28–29). These few traits summarize Zazu's personality; the repetition of the word *cuerpo* reminds the reader of her nymphomania; final similes purposefully offset these undesirable characteristics by evoking pity for her apparently helpless condition.

Other physical portraits are equally vague: Soledad is briefly described as tall, thin, long-legged, with a long neck and hard mouth (*En esta tierra*); Paulina ("El tiempo") is fragile and unreal. Valba Abel has intense eyes, wolf's teeth, straight hair, and indecisive hands. The grandmother provides the only description of Matia in her despairing comments about her large mouth and wide-set eyes, one of which turns out (*Primera memoria*, p. 120–21). There are even fewer pictures of the boys, except for an occasional reference to their eyes.

The most outstanding single characteristic of adolescence is its overwhelming solitude. Unlike Matute's children, her older characters are keenly aware of their aloneness; this realization soon evolves into a conscious estrangement during the later years of adolescence and early adulthood.[1] The youths try to break through the barrier of solitude and communicate with others: tentative experiments with love, friendship, solidarity with man, end in failure. Love, once discovered, is soon destroyed, usually through death; friendships are rare, disappointing or one-sided, for one character often takes advantage of the other; an empathy with all men (an incipient social idealism characteristic of this stage) is soon frustrated as the adolescent discovers that his proffered sympathy or comradeship is completely misconceived or not returned.

Matute's unusual ability to supply a convincing picture of this unhappy condition is evident in her sensitive descriptions of the adolescent's loneliness. Matia's observation about her cousin Borja becomes a generalization on the pitiful condition of man: "(Tal vez, pienso ahora, con toda tu bravuconería, con tu soberbio y duro corazón, pobre hermano mío, ¿no eras acaso un animal solitario como yo, como casi todos los muchachos del mundo?)" (*Primera memoria*, p. 35). A passage from *Pequeño teatro* repeats key words (*sola, gritos*) to heighten the keen despair of Zazu's loneliness: "Una gran soledad se ceñía enteramente a ella. Era en aquellos momentos cuando Zazu se sabía sola. Sola y pequeña, extrañamente débil y pequeña. . . . Zazu se veía avanzar menuda, niña, escondiendo las manos a la espalda. Había un largo túnel en su vida. Un largo túnel del que huían los pájaros, como gritos breves y agudos, como negros gritos disparados, igual que salpicaduras de tinta" (pp. 25–26). Bear's new friendship only heightens his feelings of separation: "En esos momentos, Bear se sentía desconcertado y extraordinariamente solo. Cosa rara, porque antes no tenía amigos, como ahora: y antes, nunca tuvo conciencia de su soledad" (*La trampa*, p. 34).

It is likely that Matute chose to call her main character Soledad expressly for the name's symbolic import in the novel *En esta tierra;* this girl experiences almost every kind of loneliness, alienation, or separation. Circumstances of the Civil War introduce her to a hostile world: the violent death of her father, sudden poverty, disaffection from her family, estrangement from others and especially from the attitudes of the citizens of Barcelona, all contribute to a total isolation. Her solution is to search within the confines of her loneliness: "Todo era pobre y oscuro a su alrededor, mezquino e insufi-ciente. . . . Estaba sola, profundamente sola, lejana, ence-rrada. . . . ¿Dónde habrá un lugar para mí?, se dijo con vaga melancolía. Su lugar parecía estar en sí misma, su refugio era su propio corazón" (p. 130). Soledad's deliberations signal a common trend in adolescence. The growing awareness of solitude and ideological alienation encourages the adolescent to evaluate his role in life. This examination begins with the acknowledgment of life as a vital force which offers infinite possibilities for self-realization. Life in its most uncomplicated aspects tempts Babel to cry out, "¡Es hermosa, muy hermosa, la vida! . . . ¡Cuando se es puro y simple e ignorante!" ("La frontera del pan," *El tiempo,* p. 196). A crisis may also affirm the most basic assets; *En esta tierra* pits life and love against war and death (p. 27); Soledad's brother Eduardo reacts against his fear of death by exalting life: "Se miró las venas de los brazos. Allí estaba su vida. Lo único importante para él. Lo único defendible, para él. Amaba su cuerpo, lo amó aquel día sobre todas las cosas de la tierra" (p. 83). Both pairs of rebels in *Los hijos muertos* (Daniel-Verónica, Miguel-Mónica) give a greater value to life because they recognize that others have denied it (p. 324). Pablo esteems life above all else, as he explains to his half-brother, "No hay muerte para mí. Mien-tras yo viva, no existe la muerte. . . . No existe nada antes de mí ni después de mí" (*Fiesta al noroeste,* p. 109).

61

The adolescent soon feels a necessity to continue his explorations by investigating the possibilities contained within life. "Cuánto existe que no conozco" is Valba Abel's wistful statement (*Los Abel*, p. 75), but the desire to know all facets of life is expressed directly or indirectly by all adolescents. Miguel "pensaba que el mundo era fantástico, insospechado; que el mundo y la vida eran algo misterioso y hasta aquel momento desconocido" (*Los hijos muertos*, p. 474). The desire for some vague or unknown fulfillment—usually a basic justification for life or the answer to an existential problem—is an outgrowth of the character's expanding awareness. The first acknowledgment of life thus enlarges to a more involved attitude which begins with the search for a meaning or justification for existence. It is no coincidence that the author repeatedly uses the word thirst in connection with adolescence, for it symbolizes the desire for discovery: "Entró en la edad de la sed, de los sueños de perfección" (*En esta tierra*, p. 16); "La atmósfera de su adolescencia estaba cargada de sed" (*En esta tierra*, p. 59); "Su sed no se iba a acabar. Había despertado a la sed" ("La ronda," *El tiempo*, p. 81).

Many of the young people turn their attentions upon themselves, exploring their own inner horizons, the purpose of their existence, the way to inner freedom. Some manage to see themselves rather objectively. The character may begin by questioning the purpose of his existence. In "La ronda," this process is compressed into the single night before Miguel is to leave for the war: refusing to join the rowdy drinking party in honor of the departing draftees, he remains alone in an "inner" *ronda*, which is to justify his life: "Si se nace para morirse todos los días, ¡qué simples y monstruosos le resultaban todos los actos! Pensó en su ronda, que iría reconstruyendo de lugar en lugar . . . toda su existencia. Reconstituiría su vida en pos de un solo instante que salvara todos sus años. Si se le salvaba un solo instante que lo justificara, partiría" (*El tiempo,* p. 85). The search for one's identity, an existential facet of the adolescent's development, encourages a thorough self-analysis which examines the meaning and purpose of one's place in life: "Te quedas solo. Solo, frente a ti mismo. . . . Únicamente entonces conoces tus límites y piensas: toda mi vida era únicamente un gran deseo de romperlos. . . . ¿Para qué luchar, para qué esforzarse en algo, para qué vivir y apetecer, si primero no nos liberamos de nosotros mismos, de nuestra cobardía, de nuestras claudicaciones?" (*En esta tierra,* p. 155).

A powerful, primitive metaphor much used in connection with self-discovery is that of reflection, either in a mirror or in some other reflecting object. Valba Abel's "autobiography" is punctuated with mirror-images, each revealing a new phase of development: her search for identity begins with a self-encounter: "Me miré en un espejo. . . . No sabía qué esperaban de mí" (*Los Abel,* pp. 35–36); her desire for freedom and a new kind of life starts with the mirror image ("De pronto me vi reflejada en el agua . . . y sentí una rara expectación, y como un hálito de vida nueva" (p. 62). Her first introduction to Jacqueline includes a strange experience as Valba glances into a mirror: "De pronto me golpeó mi propia imagen, reflejándose en un espejo. Me sentí extraña a ella, desproporcionadamente distinta" (p. 94). The end of the novel and another reflection show Valba's hopeless bitterness: "A menudo iba yo chocando con mi imagen reflejada en los espejos. Y mi imagen llegó a obsesionarme" (pp. 212–13). This device also serves as a presage when she is forced to tell her brother that he will be permanently lame, and she symbolically destroys their reflected images in the water (p. 108). Both Mónica and Miguel experience self-revelation as they look at themselves in the mirror (*Los hijos muertos,* pp. 311, 374); Zazu realizes the truth about herself after staring into her reflection (*Pequeño teatro,* pp. 262–63). Matia's mirror discloses her solitude, a sense of unreality, and the desire to escape: "Nubes de vapor que empañaban el espejo y le daban un aire aún más irreal y misterioso. 'Alicia en el mundo del espejo,' pensé, más de una vez, contemplándome en él, desnuda y desolada, con un gran deseo de atravesar su superficie, que parecía gelatinosa. Tristísima imagen aquella . . . la imagen misma de la soledad" (*Primera memoria*, p. 73).

This self-exploration may include a glance backward into the past at "el niño que no ha muerto ni está en ninguna parte,"[2] or forward to envision future ideals, but the main search is more inclusive in nature, for it is in the image of contemporary man that the adolescent must find himself. As an extension of the mirror image, the youth may also find all or part of himself mirrored in others, in the discovery of common bonds (of suffering, of affection, of camaraderie) between himself and all men. Sympathetic attraction now supersedes introspection as the youth employs different means to communicate with others.

The character's quest for friendship symbolizes his effort to break the limitations of his own personality. Potential friendship may arise from common bonds of loneliness or unhappiness; this is the case with the cousins Matia and Borja, who depend on each other for entertainment, although with a mutual wariness, and with Matia and Manuel, Victor and Miguel Bruno ("La ronda"), and Eduardo and the gang (*En esta tierra*), among others. Each of these attempts at friendship, however, proves abortive; disinterest is misunderstood and the stronger invariably takes advantage of the weaker.

On a larger scale, the experience of love repeats the failure of friendship to provide a solution. Matia's bitter comment "Acaso, sólo deseaba que alguien me amara alguna vez. No lo recuerdo bien" (*Primera memoria*, p. 83) sets the general tone of the adolescent's quest. A mutual need draws the adolescents together in a desperate attempt to find themselves.

Once joined by love, there is neither need nor desire to express their affection aloud. Silence, in this case, is not a lack of communication, but rather the complement to a deep understanding that needs no words.

The physical aspect of love, although not unduly emphasized, is not omitted from these works. In *Primera memoria,* the discovery of sex increases Matia's feeling of disgust for adult values. Her descriptions, therefore, employ physical or sexual references to emphasize her repugnance: "Era espeso y obsceno aquel cuarto, como el gran vientre y los pechos de tía Emilia" (*Primera memoria,* p. 125). Her attitude causes her to cry out in anguish, "No, no me descubras más cosas, no me digas oscuras cosas de hombres y mujeres, porque no quiero saber nada del mundo que no entiendo. Déjame, déjame, que aún no lo entiendo" (*Primera memoria,* pp. 143–44). Feelings of fear, terror, and shame, accompany Matia's awakening to adulthood and heighten the tone of aversion to all that adults represent which colors her attitude. In *En esta tierra,* Eduardo's memories of an evening spent with two girls also include the same kind of ambivalent feelings toward sexual love, in a nightmare of arms like tentacles and melting, viscous mouths (p. 101). In a reversed situation, Zazu's nymphomania has roots that would fascinate the modern psychiatrist: she uses love to search for the meaning of her existence and as an escape mechanism (*Pequeño teatro,* pp. 41, 263).

Yet, love may also solve the adolescent's problems; companionship and mutual understanding offset loneliness or unhappiness. This thought prompts Soledad to feel that love compensates for the burden of daily struggle (*En esta tierra,* p. 128); it also transforms the barren existence of Pedro: "Junto a Paulina, todas las cosas eran nuevas, estaban llenas de sangre, de fe. . . . Por vez primera, algo le arrancaba de la sórdida tristeza, de la desesperanza. Comprendió de pronto el porqué de las cosas, el porqué de los hombres. Como un milagro se abrió ante él un mundo apretado de esperanzas" ("El tiempo," *El tiempo,* pp. 64–65).

Valba Abel's memoirs record her attempts to adapt her ideas about love to reality. Eloy's courtship, marked by a total lack of communication, does not measure up to her idealistic notions about love: "El amor era el principio de la vida, y parecía extraño que el amor de Eloy me apagase y me matara" (*Los Abel,* p. 99). She finally rejects Eloy, leaves home, and becomes involved with Galo, an older man, whose love seems to satisfy her desire to live life to the fullest. Galo's subsequent desertion coincides with the abandonment of her own hopes for happiness, and she returns home with the realization of her failure in both love and life: "Si algún día volvía a amar, mi sentimiento arrastraría un coro de burlas y parodias. O tal vez mi corazón estaba por fin seco" (p. 207).

According to an invariable pattern, love inevitably comes to a tragic end. Most couples are separated by premature death: Cristián-Soledad (*En esta tierra*), Daniel-Verónica and Miguel-Mónica (*Los hijos muertos*), Pedro and Paulina ("El tiempo," *El tiempo*); others by circumstances beyond their control (Pablo and his fiancée [*Fiesta al noroeste*]), or by a misunderstanding ("La frontera de pan," *El tiempo*). Zazu kills herself, fighting against her attraction to Marco (*Pequeño teatro*); Valba leaves Eloy and is in turn deserted by Galo. Love may be a step in self-discovery, but it obviously is not the self-revelation it appears to be at first.

The strong ties of blood relationships, which at first seem excessive, are still another way of relating one's own existence to that of others. Valba Abel's reactions typify this attitude, for she transcends her own image by fusing it with that of her brothers: "Si me gustaba mirar a través de cada uno de mis hermanos, ¿por qué limitarme tan sólo mi imagen en el espejo? Sentía a mis hermanos como a mi sangre. . . . Como si fuera yo un poco de cada uno, como si todos ellos tuvieran algo de mí" (*Los Abel,* p. 56). Juan Medinao, drawn to his half-brother by ambivalent feelings of love and hatred, expresses the same idea (*Fiesta al noroeste*, p. 111).[3]

A final part of the adolescent's self-analysis is his feeling of solidarity with man: an identification with all men, in whom the adolescent recognizes a duplication of his own traits.[4] Although other works contain brief references to this expansion of personality, notably a phrase by Valba Abel as she watches the town church burn to the ground ("Hubiera querido incrustarme en cada alma, una a una, y sentir en cada cuerpo una sangre distinta," *Los Abel*, p. 116), Daniel (*Los hijos muertos*) provides the greatest insights into the theme. His rejection of the values of his own people to support the masses, to whom he feels drawn by "bonds of alliance," is the irrevocable commitment to others, to whom he promises allegiance: "Sí, sí, allí dentro de él, como estrellas nacidas, ascendían voces en su mente de muchacho aún ignorante. Era su tiempo de esperanza. . . . Se sentía marcado, predestinado. Su rebeldía, su esperanza, se encendían y crecían. . . . 'Me iré de aquí, salvaré a los míos.' Tenía catorce, quince, dieciséis años. Tenía la fuerza de la primera fe" (pp. 71–72).

A strong social preoccupation, which is a constant in Ana María Matute's books, may accompany the latter part of the adolescent's search, in which the feeling of empathy combines with idealistic intentions to better the life of man. The adolescent now reaches the peak of his development; his disinterest allows him to submerge his individuality in an attempt to help others. Each is willing to sacrifice himself in some way for the benefit of man or to further the cause he believes in: Daniel joins the *republicanos;* Cristián and Soledad envision a better future; Pablo works with the people first as a teacher and later as a leader in the revolution; Babel links his life with a girl he intends to help; Manuel and Marta literally sacrifice themselves for their beliefs; and Bear repeats the same kind of gratuitous self-sacrifice a generation later (*La trampa*).

At this point, the adolescent finds a justification for his

existence in his idealism: "Algo, entonces, vibraba intensa-
mente en su dolor. Algo que le decía: los hombres no se
apagan. Era preciso nacer un poco en cada instante, hallar un
rincón donde no existiesen patrullas a la caza de muchachos
que aún tienen que vivir. Si ese lugar no existía, era necesario
crearlo, ser de los que amasan una época que no tuviese nada
que ver con las ciudades encendidas ni con las ciudades que se
esconden en la noche" (*En esta tierra*, p. 150). He is willing
to fight for what he believes in: Daniel Corvo, in his "tiempo
de esperanza," as the author calls this stage, also feels com-
pelled to help others. It is his great faith that enables the
adolescent to overcome or overlook the constant obstacles:
" 'Tiempo de seguridad, de fe.' La gran fuerza, la confianza,
empujándole a través del hambre, de la apatía, de la desesperanza de los otros, de la amoralidad o la indiferencia de los
otros, empujándole a través de la injusticia, de la impiedad,
. . . el pillaje, el fatalismo" (*Los hijos muertos*, pp. 123–24).

The character's idealistic intentions and his commitment to
a goal seem to offer the fulfillment he has been seeking. This
commitment calls for action, yet the adolescent soon discovers
that his efforts, whether philanthropic or self-centered, are
fruitless. The realization of his inability to fight against forces
beyond his control marks the start of a downward trend.
Thus, if the first part of adolescence comprises a period of
expectation and discovery, the second part is a direct contrast
in the emphasis on unhappiness, fear, and ultimate disen-
chantment. The consistent final disillusionment suggests a
fatalistic view of life which preoccupies Matute enough to
appear repeatedly in her literature. A tragic aura surrounds
the adolescents, whose fate will be early death, renunciation
of society, or unhappy resignation before the inevitable. The
author carefully lays the groundwork for the tragic ending by
various portents in the form of presages and repeated references to fate. Soledad feels herself "marcada como Caín,

indefensamente empujada hacia algo que, aunque desconocido, la aterraba" (*En esta tierra*, p. 19), and when Pedro tells Paulina to put on the symbolic shoes as they escape in "El tiempo," he realizes that in speaking those words he is obeying a "fatal sign" (*El tiempo*, p. 68). Numerous references to fear help to set the mood for the adolescent's unhappy fate. A common object may symbolically represent this dread, for example, the overhead lamp in "La ronda," which sways mysteriously whenever riders pass over the mountain, and which is a constant symbol of terror: "Pero nada era para Miguel Bruno como la lámpara. Llegó a creerla un insecto de especie gigante. . . . Tenía miedo. Fue entonces cuando presintió un poder impalpable, feroz y vagamente enemigo sobre sus cabezas dobladas. Algo que flotaba, que existía más allá de su ir y venir sobre la tierra" (*El tiempo*, pp. 75–76). Others experience vague presentiments concerning the future: "Yo sabía . . . que el mundo era algo malo y grande. Y me asustaba pensar que aún podía ser más aterrador de lo que imaginaba" (*Primera memoria*, p. 106).

This fear is far from unfounded: it foreshadows incidents which will contribute to the adolescent's disaffection from society, the disappearance of his idealism, and his ultimate rejection of the world. The character slowly becomes aware of life's serious limitations; time and death, undesirable traits in society or individuals, and the final inability to adjust his ideals to reality, introduce the end of this period and the threshold of adulthood.

The adolescent's experiences soon oblige him to acknowledge the presence of antagonistic forces—life and death—which will haunt him throughout his life. The dual forces of time and death form a twin motif in Ana María Matute's works; "El tiempo," the title story in the book of the same name, symbolizes this preoccupation in its title and subject matter. The train's piercing whistle is a symbol of time itself:

its shrill sound regularly punctuates the story, reminding Pedro of the passage of time (p. 51). It runs down the two protagonists as they are escaping from time and loneliness: "El grito llegó. Los atravesó. Los dejó atrás. Desaforado y frío, agujereando la niebla, el grito desapareció de nuevo tras las últimas rocas" (p. 70). Time is a destructive force which mows down everything in its path: "El tiempo que agostaba las cosas, que traía la muerte, el polvo seco del olvido, las cicatrices, las luces apagadas, las habitaciones vacías" (p. 62). The stylistic deformation of the surroundings also tends toward symbols suggesting the passage of time: the train in "El tiempo"; the constant strumming of a guitar in "La ronda," which reminds Miguel of a clock that obsessively crumbles the night (p. 89); the fountain in "La frontera de pan," which seems to tell Babel that he will die just as his forefathers did (p. 187).

Each character must eventually acknowledge the power and malevolent aspects of time; each experiences the same sense of uneasiness when thinking about it. Valba reflects, "Los años galopaban como los minutos; yo me quedaría un día muerta en un camino" (*Los Abel*, p. 201); Soledad remarks that time symbolizes a continual loss, causes a sense of anguish. An old photograph of her relatives evokes a similar fear in Mónica: "¿Qué ocurría con el tiempo, que quemaba las cosas, que las volvía ceniza, que pudría el amor y el afecto, el corazón, la amistad? ¿Qué ocurría con el tiempo, que deshermanaba, que mataba, que olvidaba?" (*Los hijos muertos*, p. 316).

Themes directly connected with the obsession with time also heighten the general attitude of unhappiness, fear, or foreboding. The adolescents soon realize the transitory condition of life; some, like Eduardo or Cloti (*En esta tierra*), make this awareness an excuse to live life to the fullest; contrasted with this is Soledad's feeling of helplessness before "cosas que huían irremisiblemente de su lado, sin que pudiera detener-las" (*En esta tierra,* p. 207). Death offers obvious associations with the passage of time; its presence (almost every work has one or more deaths) or the fear of impending doom haunts the characters. Still another attitude is the desire to dismiss this terrible reality as "otra de las tantas patrañas que cuentan los hombres a los muchachos" (*Primera memoria,* p. 175). With her delicate sense of effective contrast, Matute also uses death to reaffirm the positive values of life. Therefore, although Miguel Bruno says, "Parecía que realmente sólo se naciese al borde de la muerte" (*El tiempo,* p. 82), Valba Abel feels that her father's death commits her to life; and Cristián admits that the thought of death enhances life (*En esta tierra,* p. 256).

This fatalistic conception, reinforced by presages in the form of symbolic objects, vague fears, and so forth, culminates in the second part of adolescence, which presents an almost unvarying pattern of steady progression toward discourage-ment and disgust with society. Coercion by the forces of society, or compromises in conflict with his own ideals, cause the adolescent to reject gradually—either mentally or phys-ically—his citizenship in the world. The author makes this process unmistakable through a series of events by which the adolescent is made aware of the cruelty of life and is forced to acknowledge that he is little more than a misfit in society. The adolescent soon perceives the unsatisfactory condition of life: descriptions of a very brutal side of existence purpose-fully reinforce the character's feeling of estrangement. Valba's picture of a nearby town is a somber and hopeless one: "En aquel pueblo nuestro trabajaban hombres y brutos abrazados a un mismo suelo, mezclado su sudor. Ni una máquina, ni un descanso, ni una dulzura. . . . Bebían, bebían: todo lo apaga-ban en el chorro amoratado de la bota. Su suciedad era turbia como su ambición, su desesperanza" (*Los Abel,* p. 59). The sack of Barcelona, in which "la brutalidad parecía atenuada por el silencio" (*En esta tierra,* p. 286), is no less revealing in its undesirable aspects. *Los hijos muertos* is filled with detailed descriptions or lengthy enumerations of the miseries suffered by the poor. The impact of privation, hunger, and apathy complements the adolescent's dissatisfaction with society.

The primary cause of the adolescent's disillusionment, however, is human nature. His extreme solitude, the hopelessness of trying to communicate with others, and especially the inevitable egotism that surrounds him make the adolescent strive to dissociate himself completely from society. This feeling prompts Mónica to exclaim, " 'Mundo asqueroso éste, de viejos cansados por todas partes, dejándonos morir a nosotros, así, a su lado.' La rabia le subía, despaciosa y fría, otra vez. Empezaba a conocer el odio" (*Los hijos muertos,* p. 497). Pedro also feels himself trapped by "toda la incomprensión y la espantosa sensatez que los rodeaba" ("El tiempo," *El tiempo,* p. 65). Bear's whole attitude stems from his disaffection from present conditions, typified by the rigid, meaningless forms of adult society: "El mundo se había convertido en una sucesión de frases cáscara, absolutamente hueras. . . . Para concretar, el viejo mundo le pareció sucio y pequeño" (*La trampa,* p. 45).

Because of the unwillingness with which he receives these conditions, the adolescent's feelings range from melancholy and vague disturbance, to complete unhappiness. Some of the most poignant sections in *Primera memoria* describe Matia's distress at the knowledge that she cannot remain a child and must, despite herself, enter a world she does not choose to accept. Matute captures the anguish of having to admit an irrevocable change: "Y yo estaba a punto de crecer y de convertirme en una mujer. . . . No, no, que esperen un poco más . . . un poco más.' Pero ¿quién tenía que esperar? Era yo, sólo yo, la que me traicionaba a cada instante. . . . '¿Qué clase de monstruo soy ahora . . . que ya no tengo mi niñez y no soy, de ninguna manera, una mujer?' " (*Primera memoria*, p. 148). Valba's feeling of unhappiness is more vague than that of Matia, but is more indicative of the state of mind of these adolescents: "Y a mi pesar, estaba despertándome una tristeza, una rebeldía, que luchaban entre sí y me arrancaba un dolor profundo, desconocido" (*Los Abel*, p. 73). Pedro of "El tiempo" is also typical of the general attitude of uneasiness (*El tiempo*, pp. 54–55) or the genuine feeling of anguish so common in the last stages of adolescence.

The limitations which the adolescent encounters alienate him from society; the premonition of failure or impending tragedy accompanies the experiences he undergoes. Matute makes the reader fully aware of the disillusionment, disgust, or denial which the protagonist may feel toward society. For Matia, recognition of the detested adult world comes in a series of sudden, sharp intuitions triggered by the treacherous acts of Borja: "En aquel momento me hirió el saberlo todo. (El saber la oscura vida de las personas mayores, a las que, sin duda alguna, pertenecía [yo] ya. Me hirió y sentí un dolor físico)" (*Primera memoria*, p. 239).

This acknowledgment, however, does not always follow a terrible event; it is more often the result of an accumulation of petty incidents which finally weigh too heavily on the protagonist. Pedro, for example, recognizes "cuán sórdida y falta de esperanza era su vida. Atado a aquella mesa de trabajo, a un trabajo que no le satisfacía . . . solamente podía aspirar a no morir de hambre ni de frío" ("El tiempo," *El tiempo*, p. 52). Soledad, who finally discovers the limitations of mankind (p. 46), also gives voice to a theory of the needlessness of human existence: "Sobraban hombres por todas partes, hombres innecesarios y míseros, que nadie se explicaba por qué crecían y se alistaban en las filas del hambre, con deseos de continuar viviendo" (*En esta tierra*, p. 47).[5] Cloti, even more pessimistic, believes that "La vida era una mentira inmensa, monstruosa. Nadie ayuda a nadie, nadie lucha por nadie" (*En esta tierra*, p. 113).

Daniel's experiences trace clearly the trajectory from idealism to disillusionment. Social idealism determines his commitment. He breaks with his family and joins the *republicanos*: "Llegaba, ahora, para él un tiempo de acción. Estaba preparado. Lleno de voluntad y de fe" (*Los hijos muertos*, p. 112). Even the battles do not diminish his optimistic attitude because, as he states, it is difficult to kill hope (p. 185). During the last days of the war he finally is forced to recognize the absurdity of everything, including his own cause (p. 188). His flight to France and the death of Verónica end his dreams for social reform and personal happiness, and he leaves Spain symbolically abandoning all hope. The failure of his own efforts and his bitter outlook completely color his attitude: "Ahora, sólo sentía el final. El final de un mundo. Algo había terminado. . . . Era el fin de un mundo, de una esperanza, de una idea de la vida" (p. 297).

Most other adolescents in Matute's works duplicate Daniel's failure: they must acknowledge defeat through failure to accomplish a determined goal, the impossibility of their ideals, the loss of love or death of a beloved, or the inability to adjust to society. Most end their adolescence with a greater sense of deprivation, solitude, or failure than they began with. A few examples will suffice: Pablo's unsuccessful dreams of his "promised land"; Matia's sense of horror at having betrayed her only friend; Daniel's total failure (discussed above); Babel's frustrated attempts to help another ("La frontera del pan"); Valba Abel's double loss of her brothers and her lover.

By emphasizing these traits, Ana María Matute successfully describes a period of life which is full of promise during the early stage but ends in bitterness and despair. Before acknowledging defeat, however, the adolescents, fully conscious of what is happening to them, fiercely rebel against the injustices they experience. Recognizing that they cannot accept life as it is, several young characters go through a similar evolution: a feeling of being trapped, a subsequent desire for liberty, rebellion against the social order, and finally, escape. A reference to the word chains symbolizes Pedro's subordination to society and its routine: "Deseaba violentamente liberarse de tantas ligaduras como le sujetaban. Se sabía preso de cosas irremediables, vulgares cosas irremediables, que no tenía derecho ni fuerza para cortar. Y sabía que, a medida que fuera haciéndose hombre, estas cadenas más y más le apresarían, y más y más iba a serle imposible romperlas" ("El tiempo," *El tiempo,* p. 25). Valba Abel also uses the same word (*cadenas*) to describe the oppressiveness of her environment (*Los Abel,* p. 60).

The increasing disgust which the character feels toward society, certain individuals, or distasteful situations causes his revolt. Valba, contemplating the love that Eloy has to offer, says, "yo no quería apagarme lentamente en su vivir en declive. . . . Mientras fuera posible le huiría" (*Los Abel,* p. 90), and Matia, who from the first pages of *Primera memoria* has been rebelling against both the adult world and her own inevitable growth, suddenly voices her resistance to adult values after someone poisons Manuel's water supply: "De pronto, me levanté de entre todo aquello. Era solamente yo" (p. 135). *Los hijos muertos* is fraught with undercurrents of tension and rebellion which run through the generations described. Daniel goes against his family and joins "los de abajo"; Verónica leaves her family to join Daniel; Miguel, weaned on the rebellions of the Civil War, turns against society in unlawful action and refuses to accept the consequences of his imprisonment; Mónica rejects the older generation, personified by Isabel, which refuses to understand her.

75

The desire for freedom is a natural consequence of this attitude, and is found not only in Miguel's physical escape from the prison (*Los hijos muertos*), but also in the attempts of the adolescents to free themselves from the oppression of society and all that surrounds them. The final result of this cycle is the rejection of the world, but the theme of escape assumes a different meaning from what it had in childhood, although the methods of escape—physical, mental, or suicidal—often coincide with those of the children. The desire to leave one's home or community usually includes some symbolic significance: Pedro's escape from his town ("El tiempo") is actually a flight from time, which ultimately destroys him; Valba's move to the city is a rejection of the values of her family, as well as of Eloy's love; Daniel, Verónica, and Mónica run to the woods from Isabel, who embodies rigid traditional values; Miguel's wish to escape from prison is likewise a rejection of the society which condemned him for rebelling in the first place.

Several adolescents, however, manage to escape in other ways, notably in the mental renunciation of the adult world. The wish to return to the safe world of childhood is one manifestation of the rejection of a dangerous and incomprehensible world. The best example of this is *Primera memoria*. Matute shows exceptional sensitivity in portraying this intermediate stage, in stressing the unwillingness with which Matia accepts the fact that she is no longer a child: " 'Oh, no, no, detenedme, por favor. Detenedme, yo no sabía hacia dónde corría, no quiero conocer nada más' " (p. 163). Juan Medinao's hypocritical renunciation of the world for religion, is, in effect, a clever means of evading life and its responsibilities.

The last type of escape is the rejection of life itself, an extreme solution used by some troubled adolescents. In *Pequeño teatro*, Zazu drowns herself. Another character sacrifices himself in a unique rebellion ("No hacer nada"): "Pensó una vez más cuánto cuesta vivir, cuántas cosas se precisan para vivir. Y se dijo: 'Pues bien: ¿Para qué diablos esta vida?' " (*El tiempo,* p. 219). He commits suicide by going to the woods, lying down under a tree, and simply doing nothing—a silent repudiation of what he considers to be a false type of life.

To these deaths must be added the great number of adolescents who die by means other than suicide.[6] Whether by accidental death, self-sacrifice, murder, or some other means, the mortality rate of the adolescents is exceptionally high: Pedro, Miguel, and Martín (*El tiempo*); Cristián, Daniel (*En esta tierra*); Miguel and Verónica (*Los hijos muertos*); Manuel and Marta of *Los soldados lloran de noche.* Thus death (accidental, intentional self-sacrifice, or suicide), a rejection of society, or a sense of futility and failure end the cycle of the adolescent most commonly re-created by Ana María Matute's works.

The strong sense of dualism evident in every aspect of Matute's literature appears here as well. As in childhood, the contrast between objective reality and subjective emotions, idealism, and egotism is evident. There is also an important dualism of character in the opposition between the special adolescent and other youths who do not possess the former's heightened awareness. The variation in character reinforces the idealism, hope, or sensitivity of the first group by contrast with more selfish attitudes. The girls of Oiquixa fall into the latter category: "Eran hijas de familias acomodadas de Oiquixa, jovencitas de mirada incierta y pequeñas bocas movibles, chillonas, como agujerillos malignos e inocentes. Con sus tremendas horas vacías, sus largos aburrimientos de hijas de Kale Nagusia. Dentro de sus vestidos de colores vivos, como gritos en el aburrimiento largo de las casas confortables. Dentro de las tardes grises y llenas de polvo del domingo.

Como violentos chillidos amarillos, rojos, verdes, en el denso paseo de la mañana, tras la Misa en San Pedro. Como tristes y lánguidos gritos inútiles, azules, rosa, malva, en el atardecer tan paseado, Kale Nagusia arriba, Kale Nagusia abajo. Desgranando palabras, desgranando pequeñas envidias inocentes, feroces envidias adolescentes, tiernas envidias ignorantes. . . . Eran tres muchachas buenas, acechadas por maldades y crueldades monstruosamente pequeñas, atravesadas de palabras como alfileres de cabeza negra, palabras agudas y negras, necias palabras rebosantes de maligna inocencia" (*Pequeño teatro*, p. 33). The author's masterful union of form and content is evident in this passage. The slow rhythm of the prose (through the accumulation of adjectives, metaphors, and prepositional phrases) intensifies the impression of boredom in the girls' lives. Implicit or expressed antitheses throughout (*malignos, inocentes; colores vivos, tardes grises; maldades y crueldades monstruosamente pequeñas; maligna inocencia*) offer violent contrasts, and the fragmentary sentences complement the total impression of pettiness which marks their lives.

Other, more individualized characters contrast with the special group because of their selfishness or egotism. In this class are Eduardo and Cloti (*En esta tierra*), Miguel (*Los hijos muertos*), and Borja (*Primera memoria*). The attitudes of Miguel and Cloti are understandable; their common backgrounds of poverty and insecurity have molded their characters; to take advantage of others is a natural consequence of their early life. Borja and Eduardo come from better families; they have no reason to behave as they do, yet the author does not clarify their actions by showing any character evolution. Eduardo, the less offensive of the two, is a near hedonist, lacking any feeling of responsibility toward family or society, an individual who "se sabía abúlico, frío, lejano a todo aquello. . . . Le empujaba únicamente un recelo egoísta del mundo y de los hombres. La familia se le antojaba un peso aplastante" (*En esta tierra*, p. 75). Borja, on the other hand, is a consummate hypocrite, cruel, completely lacking in sensitivity. Matute ironically juxtaposes his sanctimoniousness with his very unchristian attitude by using religious references when describing him: "Borja se persignaba, el rosario entre sus dedos dorados, como un frailecito. Eso parecía, con sus desnudos pies castaños dentro de las sandalias" (*Primera memoria*, p. 23). This is doubly effective since Borja later makes use of the confession to have Manuel unjustly sent to reform school.

Daniel summarizes this type of adolescent in the following comment: "Ya no se pierden los chicos por sus sueños, por su fe, por su rebeldía. Ya no se pierden los chicos por su esperanza" (*Los hijos muertos*, p. 468). Nevertheless, Ana María Matute does not condemn the characters of this group; her tenderness encompasses children and adolescents of all types.

To convey the precise relationship between the adolescent and his environment demands a different kind of style from that which describes the dreamlike atmosphere of the children. For the most part, Matute discards the flowery images of childhood and espouses a style closely allied to "the realistic." Since the realistic technique is not used chronologically but alternates with other styles, depending on the nature of the material, it is obvious that the interplay between poetic prose and realism is not experimental but a deliberate attempt to correlate new content with an appropriate style. This style, however, is not realism in the nineteenth-century manner, but a modern adaptation of a traditional mode: a highly selective, stylized form, specifically tailored to express the adolescent's point of view and to heighten stylistically his feelings, revealing his inner self through language. Matute forces the reader to empathize with the adolescent and to understand his outlook on the world by expressing it exclusively from his limited viewpoint. This she accomplishes by selecting a narrow focus on life (that of the adolescent) which complements and often explains the mood, feelings, and convictions of the protagonist without the necessity of intrusion by the author. Therefore, although the style rests on a realistic basis, its selective and suggestive stylization approaches impressionism or expressionism.

Although the reader may not be given a complete description of the adolescent himself, he does receive detailed impressions of the outside world directly through the eyes of the character. Increased sensorial metaphors imply a physical as well as a mental awakening to his surroundings, yet such details stray from realistic prose because of the intense emotional focus which subjectively colors the object described. People, places, landscapes, even commonplace objects undergo a deformation through the eyes of the adolescent.

Descriptions of other characters also contain the adolescent's evaluation of the person in question. The youth rivets his attention on one part of the body, which is intensified and distorted out of all proportion with reality but which contains a subtle symbolism or association with some characteristic which has impressed the adolescent. During a rowdy celebration following the murder of a storekeeper, a priest, and other people of the middle and upper classes, Miguel can see only mouths chewing and shouting (*Los hijos muertos,* p. 227). Hands become the grotesque symbol of a former schoolmaster who tries to make love to Soledad: "Sentía resbalar sobre su cuerpo aquella mano y le pareció que crecía monstruosamente en peso, en calor, envolviéndola totalmente" (*En esta tierra,* p. 129). Alone with a boy, Matia notes that she is both obsessed and repelled by his hand (*Primera memoria,* p. 82). The focus on a single part of the body (usually the hands) imparts a feeling of repugnance and distorts reality by making it grotesquely disproportionate with the rest of the person.

Further deformation, reminiscent of a device Matute uses in the treatment of childhood, is prevalent in the equation of humans with dolls, marionettes, and other inanimate objects, another way to complement the feelings of the protagonist. For Valba Abel, life disconnected from her family seems unreal and meaningless. With this frame of mind, she refers to her friend Jacqueline as a faded doll (*Los Abel*, p. 152), or a forgotten doll (p. 186), and says that Jacqueline's mother reminds her of "una de esas máquinas de feria que arrojan sentencias y proverbios por una moneda" (p. 153). Dehuman- ization may be an attempt to depreciate unacceptable situa- tions in *En esta tierra*. The man who tries to make love to Soledad uses crutches and seems like a puppet on a string (p. 129); the ideological separation between Soledad and her brother causes her to compare him with an absurd, false, infinitely small doll (p. 142). The sounds of a family dressing a corpse seem false, like the actions of the guignol puppets (p. 204). Several references to the island in *Primera memoria*, unsupportable in all aspects to Matia, reinforce her rejection of that world as false and unreal: "Allí estaría [la abuela], como un dios panzudo y descascarillado, como un enorme y glotón muñecazo, moviendo los hilos de sus marionetas. Desde su gabinete, las casitas de los colonos con sus luces amarillas . . . eran como un teatro diminuto" (p. 60). The diminution of the island is a literary device to emphasize the different perspective of the sensitive adolescent. Animal sym- bolism also provides metaphors or similes to express the char- acter's distaste. The malevolent grandmother of *Primera me- moria* calls to Matia's mind ferocious, long-toothed animals (p. 183), and Es Marine's hand seems like an enormous crab (p. 100). The adolescent's translation of his reactions to his surroundings results in the grotesquely stylized descrip- tions which are actually a literary parallel of his alienation. The first presages of the world as an absurd and grotesque place come in the form of these descriptions, which the protagonist provides with the eyes of inexperience and through the perspective of his emotions.

The recurrent parallel between the adolescent and animals is another stylistic reinforcement of his disaffection with society and unwillingness to comply with its norms. The symbol of the wolf predominates here, perhaps because of its wildness, its complete hostility to man, and the fear it inspires. The comparison of the protagonist with animals may also be a symbol of his actual rebellion against society, or in Daniel's case, of rejection of the type of society that his family represents: "El día entero lo pasó solitario, como un lobo, hambriento, perdido, comido por el odio y el deseo de venganza. 'Estoy contra vosotros.'. . . Cuando volvió a La Encrucijada era ya de noche otra vez. Los ojos le brillaban como a los lobos" (*Los hijos muertos,* p. 78). Mónica, who echoes this attitude one generation later, draws another parallel in her first meeting with Miguel, as she observes that they both resemble wolves (*Los hijos muertos,* p. 253). Juan Medinao's half-brother, who also rebels against the fatalistic way of life, is described as a wolf or a savage animal (*Fiesta al noroeste,* pp. 66, 70). The parallel deaths of Miguel and the wolf, artistically protracted for greater impact, are the most obvious example (*Los hijos muertos,* pp. 552–53).[7]

This animal symbolism is subtly conveyed and indicates the type of character this person is to have: freedom-loving, unable to accept the pressures imposed by society, and finally, unwilling to adjust or conform to the demands of family and surroundings. These are the rebels whose idealistic convictions of adolescence are slowly broken down until they assume the bitter role of the adult.

Ana María Matute's world of adolescence concentrates on the development and analysis of character. Her novels and short stories use plot complications to complement a consistent idea of this stage of life translated into fiction. The basic pessimism prevalent throughout these works manifests itself very strongly, for the presages as well as the outcomes prove that solitude, social pressures, the necessity for compromise, and the realization of the imperfection of man will cause the adolescent's estrangement from society. Therefore it is not surprising to note that most of the adolescents end their lives or are killed as a direct or indirect result of their beliefs. The fate of those who do not die is left to the reader's imagination, but the ambiguous endings of such works as *Los Abel, En esta tierra, Primera memoria,* and "La frontera del pan" point to a very bleak, unhappy existence. Those who continue into adulthood, notably Isabel and Daniel of *Los hijos muertos,* Pablo Barral of *En esta tierra,* and Juan Medinao of *Fiesta al noroeste,* represent a logical conclusion to the disillusionment of the adolescent.

4. *Adulthood*—Una vejez espiritual

Ana María Matute once classified her own works as *desagradables* and explained this with the following statement: "Elegí la literatura como el medio para mí más idóneo y eficaz de comunicar a los hombres mi idea de ellos y de decirles mi solidaridad en su dolor de vivir."[1] The depiction of the *dolor de vivir* is the most vivid in her treatment of the adult character, who expresses feelings of disgust toward himself and his fellow man, and displays a deliberate lack of emotional involvement, a self-imposed absence of ideological or social commitment, an apathetic recognition of the unsatisfactory conditions of life, and an impression of total solitude, reinforced by an awareness of the passage of time. Attitudes ranging from disillusionment to pessimism form the one-sided adult personality. The few adults described in Matute's works are the living consequences of the experiences of her children and adolescents.[2] The fatalistic dichotomy between the adult character's view of reality and the true relationship between himself and the world has forced him to regard his existence as purposeless or absurd.

Ana María Matute's adult characters are few and generally show similar traits. The works of most interest to an examination of this subject are *Los hijos muertos,* in which the adults Isabel, Daniel, and Diego Herrera appear; one section of *En esta tierra* (the account of Pablo Barral's tragic life); *La trampa,* which deals with the adulthood and old age of characters introduced in *Primera memoria;* and several short stories, such as "Vida nueva" (*El tiempo*) or "El maestro" (*El arrepentido*). *Los hijos muertos* will form the basis of this chapter; briefer analyses of the other characters will then reveal

84

the same major traits of adulthood first shown in the characters of *Los hijos muertos*.

The author does not emphasize the traumatic aspects of the change from adolescence to adulthood so strongly as she does the childhood-adolescence separation. The end of adolescence already bears the marks of defeat, making the initiation into adulthood less abrupt. Furthermore, Matute presents most of her adults full grown, ignoring for the most part the psychological effects of this change. Where the character's literary life spans the two periods, however, there is a clear attempt to mark the beginning of adulthood. Daniel Corvo's sense of failure (*Los hijos muertos*, p. 167) causes an emotional reaction which ages him more than his years would suggest (p. 187). The final recognition of his defeat and the end of a world— the symbol of his youth and idealism—accompanies his flight to France at the end of the Civil War: "Parecía un muchacho. . . . Pero era un viejo. . . . Antes tuvo miedo, quizás. Ahora, sólo sentía el final. El final de un mundo. Algo había terminado. 'Otros vendrán, después.' Pero él estaba en el centro de un fracaso. En el fin. Era el fin de un mundo, de una esperanza, de una idea de la vida" (p. 297).

The violence of this period in history, the horror of battle, the panicked mass exodus from Spain, the terror, the disgust, and the awareness of one's absolute solitude do not cause Daniel's crisis but are rather a cleverly planned backdrop which harmonizes with the traumatic psychological change taking place: the defeat of the *republicanos* mirrors on a large scale the defeat of Daniel's efforts to help those in need.

The transition to adulthood occurs because of the consciousness of the insuperable distance between reality and idealistic or impossible goals. Isabel Corvo, for example, ages rapidly when she sacrifices herself to take charge of her home and family: "Isabel se endureció, envejeció extrañamente. Era una vejez espiritual, una vejez de expresión, de gesto, de voz, cuando aún permanecían las mejillas tersas y el cuerpo indómito" (*Los hijos muertos,* p. 26). Isabel has become an adult before her time; in this case, as in others, the normal chronological divisions between periods of life are not relevant to the characterization. The initiation into adulthood, for example, is a spiritual aging caused by factors that have nothing to do with physical growth.

The characterization of the adults who play secondary roles is limited to a few salient and undesirable traits. Juan Padre is a spendthrift and a drunkard (*Fiesta al noroeste,* p. 36); Eskarne Antía of *Pequeño teatro* is tall, bony, hard-eyed, and "tenía algo cruel y reseco, algo dañino y limpio, como el filo de un cuchillo" (p. 69). Main characters, such as Daniel or Isabel, have almost no physical identification; their emotional or psychological attitudes form the only basis for their description.

Matute's adult is conditioned by isolation, by his painful awareness of the full extent of his separateness and his inability—or refusal—to overcome his loneliness by communication with another. Each character moves through the years in total solitude. His personal sense of defeat creates a barrier built on the worst kind of loneliness: "la soledad del hombre perdido" (*Los hijos muertos,* p. 259). Interposed between men are the factors which contribute to their spiritual isolation: the ghosts of the past, which the adult cannot or will not exorcise. Diego Herrera must admit the existence of solitude, in spite of the humanitarian faith which he still possesses: "¡De todas las criaturas de la tierra únicamente el hombre está solo!" (*Los hijos muertos,* p. 190). Daniel later echoes these very words, ironically recalling them to his "friend."

A variation on this theme is the motif of the individual alone in a crowd. Even within great masses of people who share his predicament, his beliefs, or his goals, the character feels his total remoteness, the inability to communicate or even empathize with others. Daniel's admission of defeat accompanies this strange sensation: "La carretera estaba invadida de hombres, de mujeres y de niños, y, sin embargo, no hubo nunca para él imagen mayor de soledad humana. Todos y cada uno de aquellos hombres avanzaban, absolutamente solos, en el amanecer" (*Los hijos muertos*, p. 202).[3]

The rare attempts at friendship generally miscarry; satisfactory communication between men seems impossible. Therefore, when Diego calls Daniel *amigo*, the latter "se calló, pero deseaba decirle: 'No hay amigos ni hay nada, viejo loco, viejo soñador, viejo ridículo' " (*Los hijos muertos*, p. 282). Daniel has the same thoughts as they sit opposite each other at a table: "Es curioso: siempre nos sentamos uno frente a otro, nunca uno al lado del otro. Siempre ponemos algo entre los dos. . . . Caminamos también uno delante del otro" (p. 463). If friendship between men of the same age is unlikely, companionship between generations is inconceivable: in addition to the age difference, a dissimilar ideology obstructs efforts toward understanding. The younger generation has not shared the decisive experiences which formed the attitude of the adult—for example, the Civil War: "Los hijos ya no eran como los padres. Los hijos pensaban en otras cosas. Tendrían proyectos distintos, experiencias amparadas en el fracaso de ellos. Sí: los hijos miraban hacia otro punto, con ideas nuevas dentro de sus cabezas misteriosas, hoscas" (*Los hijos muertos*, p. 291). The faith or ideals which the adult remembers from his own youth seem to be lacking in the younger generation. Diego explains this to Miguel as he says, "Yo respeto la fe, la esperanza en algo mejor, y tú no tienes fe ni esperanza. Ése es tu único mal" (*Los hijos muertos*, p. 231).

A constant awareness of the many imperfections of life reinforces the adult's pessimistic view of his existence. Matute's younger protagonist makes the elimination of these unsatisfactory conditions his vital goal. Her adult, on the other hand, refuses to place any faith in a better future; he lives only in the present and can recognize only the forbidding and hopeless situation of the moment. Pettiness, cruelty, egotism—defects of human nature rather than of the social organism—are the outstanding faults which the adult dispiritedly observes.

The adult can see only limited courses of action (or none at all) in the apparently hopeless situation. He begins with a reevaluation of his position, a self-scrutiny, typical of his tendency toward introspection instead of action, consisting of tortured ruminations on past failures. But the remembrances accomplish no purpose; they neither rehabilitate the adult nor change his attitude, because the *recherche du temps perdu* is really only a masochistic reopening of old wounds.[4] His soul-searching may include a quest for that part of his personality abandoned somewhere in adolescence, perhaps his once-important goals. Daniel's unexpected effort to rescue Miguel is due in part to this kind of search: "Quizá sea que, viéndote, quiera retroceder hasta mí, a lo que ya no soy. Pero no puedo" (*Los hijos muertos*, p. 468). He even links his own fate with that of Miguel, allowing himself a glimmer of hope that he later deliberately puts out.

The adult's painstaking analysis of his past provides no solution to his present situation. He consistently arrives at the same dead ends of disillusionment, failure, and futility: "La eternidad no es para los hombres. ¡Para los hombres: paletadas de tierra, estiércol, hambre, miedo! Eso, para los hombres: tristeza, deseo y muerte. Muerte, nada más" (*Los hijos muertos*, p. 283). These memories are never pleasant, for the contrast between the past and the present is too sharp; even past happiness is colored by the foreknowledge of an unhappy future. The adult soon realizes how dangerous it is to become implicated even in his own past, and any thought of involvement is accompanied by a chilling fear: "El miedo. El miedo sin remedio. El miedo de lo que vendría, de lo que tenía que ser, sin remedio. . . . De lo que llegaría a cada paso que diera, a cada minuto que pasara" (*Los hijos muertos,* pp. 428–29). This disquietude accompanies Daniel throughout his adult life. It is not a fear of physical harm—he is totally unconcerned about his life—but an apprehension of breaking through the limits of the present in order to probe into his past, to look ahead to the future, or to relive his failure by committing himself again.[5] The adult's impassibility alters his manner of seeing reality. Life must involve nothing more than simple existence, and anything purporting to be more than this is unreal and strange. Because of this attitude, the character may even find the ideal so ardently upheld in the past to be meaningless. When Daniel remembers two women of the bourgeoisie escaping to France, he thinks, " 'Contra seres como éstos he ido yo.' (Qué extraño y absurdo resultaba todo, al fin)" (*Los hijos muertos,* p. 188).

Other experiences heighten the adult's general feelings of displacement, disharmony, and alienation. Time, for example, plays a part in enhancing the sense of absurdity and separation. Matute's child characters are unaware of time; their life is an eternal moment disconnected from traditional standards. The adolescent, although situated within the normal course of time and fully conscious of its passage, can still look toward the future for his salvation. The adult can accept neither of these interpretations, for he finds himself hopelessly entangled in another "eternal present." The past provides no meaning for his life, and he prefers to ignore the future. New situations wrought by the passage of time underscore his miserable state and ridicule his efforts to remain impassive; he is forced to watch, powerless, a replay of portions of the past brought to the present. Thus the fusion of past with present is often an ironic mockery of the adult's own life, enhancing the absurdity of events. The couple Miguel-Mónica uncannily repeats the actions of Daniel and Verónica. When Mónica rebels against Isabel and runs away from home to Daniel, he realizes that she is unconsciously mirroring Verónica's actions and attitudes: "Porque el tiempo vuelve, de improviso, cuando estamos más desamparados, más desprevenidos y confiados, porque el tiempo es un enemigo tenaz, en oleadas imprevistas, que nos arrolla con su regreso para dejarnos luego, vacíos, sedientos . . . entre nubes amarillas de polvo. El terrible polvo que el tiempo va dejando tras sí" (*Los hijos muertos*, p. 332).

Even the adult's awareness of the passage of time assumes a different tone from that of the adolescent. Daniel, for example, equates man with a "time-trap"; in his case, the retention of time within himself—trapped through memory and exhumed through constant remembrances of the past—haunts and embitters him: "Lo cierto es que el tiempo pasado está retenido en mí, como una trampa: mis viejas trampas de cazador. Sí: nos creemos hombres y sólo somos unas grandes o minúsculas trampas para detener cosas que se pierden, para que se nos pudran entre los dientes las viejas cosas que queremos detener" (p. 446).

The character's peculiar attitude causes notable modifications in his personality. The principal change is the feeling of alienation from his fellow man and an impassivity. The keynote for this is *vacío,* a word constantly reiterated or paraphrased in the case of Daniel: "Es que no puedo, es que *no soy.* Es que estoy lejos, siempre lejos. . . . Clavado en otro tiempo, quizá, o en ningún tiempo. . . . ¿En qué clase de ser me he convertido? ¿Qué se hizo de mí? No estoy con ellos, no. No estoy con los hombres, nada sé de ellos ni de sus preocupaciones. No puedo interesarme por nada de los hombres" (*Los hijos muertos*, p. 415).

The unbridgeable distance between the character and objective reality brings about his formal recognition of disillusionment: " 'Siempre igual,' pensó. La desilusión de casi todas las cosas: 'Embellecíamos demasiado la realidad. ¿Será éste, acaso, nuestro gran pecado?' " (*Los hijos muertos*, p. 301). Although Daniel Corvo formalizes this feeling, most other adults share the thought. By accepting his situation, the character tacitly admits the uselessness of rebellion against the inevitable. He does, however, destroy the last vestige of his former idealism by escaping in any of various ways, implying a rejection of life's values or of life itself. The adult's dissociation from society appears in his ideological separation from others, reinforced by actual physical remoteness, as in Daniel's seclusion in the woods. This withdrawal, carried to its greatest extreme, is a rejection of his own status as man. Daniel states, "No tengo ningún orgullo de sentirme hombre" (*Los hijos muertos*, p. 180). Daniel himself escapes through his very indifference to his surroundings: "Si despertar a la vida, era aquel grande y feroz desasosiego, aquel descontento y vacío, prefería la paz de una ausencia de sí mismo, de sus años pasados y futuros" (p. 87). The negative acceptance of his situation is his decision to move in a directionless, emotionless void. This self-imposed apathy reflects his hopelessness: "[Yo debo ser] un hombre que mire con cara de idiota a los seres y a las cosas. Cosas, viejas cosas se agolpan y galopan dentro. No, no es desesperación. Quizás es más: ausencia total de esperanza" (p. 175).

In addition to this alienation from others there appears a certain mental degeneration, that is, an *abulia* which the adult is well aware of but refuses to remedy: "Le voy a confesar una cosa: ni siquiera yo quería pensar en que podía llegar esta indiferencia. Temía mucho el día en que me acostumbrase a portarme como un perro o como un árbol. Pero, ahora, me parece bien. Sí, me parece muy bien" (*Los hijos muertos*, p. 182). This statement is characteristic of Daniel Corvo's attitude; the same feeling later prompts him to ask himself,

"¿Qué clase de animal eres, Daniel Corvo? ¿Qué horrible existencia la tuya? Ya eres un hombre muerto, Daniel Corvo. Todas las tardes te entierran en el bosque" (pp. 341–42). Finally, his admission that life is not worth living typifies the adult's attitude toward his existence: "Eso es: ir viviendo. Le juro que mi plazo me parece demasiado largo, aun en lo más escondido del bosque. . . . ¡Ir viviendo! ¡No sé qué clase de fe da usted a beber!" (*Los hijos muertos*, p. 181).

The adult's sense of disillusionment and emptiness stems in part from a certain fatalism which confirms the futility of rebelling against the inevitable. The character thus sees himself in a situation which is no longer under his control. Daniel constantly alludes to the preordained order of things with such words as "no tenía más remedio que ser como fui" (*Los hijos muertos*, p. 180), or "Bien: que sucedan las cosas como tengan que suceder. Ya no tengo ganas de luchar con lo que está marcado, quizás, en algún lugar" (p. 505).

A brief glance at two other characters in *Los hijos muertos* will show further the ubiquitous nature of man's desolation. Both are adults, contemporaries of Daniel, and their stories parallel or complement his, finally merging at the close of the novel to display the collective hopelessness of all three. Isabel Corvo is one of the few adult women treated in Matute's works. She has not dedicated herself to an abstract ideal: her whole life has been spent in a frustrated and repressed love for her cousin Daniel. It first takes the form of mother love; even she does not realize what this feeling masks until she catches Daniel and Verónica together (p. 47). The intimate bond of love and maternity is shared by others; a childless love is an unsatisfied love, for the outstanding trait of woman is motherhood. Thus in Isabel's case, lover and child fuse together in a strangely erotic image: "¡A ti, el único hijo posible para mí, el hijo que no tuve! . . . como si tu cabeza hubiera empujado con su vida mi vida, como si tu vida hubiera bañado de sangre mis muslos. Tu vida bebida por mí, respirada por mí. Daniel, Daniel, hijo mío" (*Los hijos muertos*, p. 197). When Daniel finally returns, Isabel wants to begin their relationship again, and in this light her preoccupation with time assumes a very personal meaning: "No, no es posible que el tiempo vuelva ceniza la vida. El tiempo guardará en algún lugar los años pasados, la niñez, la juventud que yo no tuve. El amor que me quemó, que me dobló la vida. ¡Ay, el tiempo pasado! ¿Sólo me quedará ya el recuerdo, la capacidad de soñar?" (p. 195). However, the ironic repetition of events already described takes place: Daniel again ignores Isabel, and she again assumes the role of accuser. "En Isabel Corvo volvía el tiempo milagroso, violento, arrastrando en remolino los viejos celos, el amor abrasado de celos salvajes, despiadados" (p. 196).

Unlike the male protagonists, Isabel is neither indifferent nor dispassionate. Although fully conscious of the failure of both purposes in her life (to restore La Encrucijada to its former status and to gain Daniel's love), she disguises any signs of despair. She still retains the domineering and enterprising ways of her youth, for the irony of her situation is that, although defeated, she has never admitted defeat. She assumes a hypocritical pose of disinterested, motherly affection toward Daniel, a role which she must continue to play throughout her life: "Pero yo vivo en pecado mortal, porque la verdad, la verdad de mi soledad, la que yo sé cuando estoy sola y desnuda de toda apariencia, nunca la dije. La verdad que yo misma me escondo, que yo misma me falseo" (p. 191).

At first glance, Diego Herrera is the only adult in Matute's works who actively struggles to keep his ideals in sight, even after terrible experiences. His penal colony, which he feels will redeem the convicts, shows an uncommonly optimistic belief in the dignity of man. Instead of allowing himself to be overwhelmed by the most horrible experience of all (seeing his son's eyes cut out by the *republicanos* before they kill him), he turns it into the nucleus of his idealism: "Creo en la sangre de mi hijo y mi hijo sigue viviendo. ¡Daniel Corvo, yo sé cómo murió él, con qué gran fe iba a la muerte! . . . yo no puedo dejarle solo, no puedo consentir que él muriese por nada" (p. 182).

His chronological age places Diego Herrera in adulthood, but his attitudes are clearly those of late adolescence: despite tragedy and obstacles, his faith in man remains firm and his goal is clearly in sight: his mission "no es otra que la de comunicar esperanza" (pp. 180–81). Miguel, a young prisoner, reminds him of his son, and thus it becomes crucial to "save" him, even in the face of the boy's distrustful egotism. Miguel's breach of faith and subsequent death mark the end of Diego's experiment and the beginning of his own sense of failure: his son has symbolically died again, taking with him Diego's humanitarian idealism: "Ha sido una calamidad. Una espantosa calamidad. Ya le digo: lo peor. Lo peor que me podía suceder. . . . Me ha hundido" (p. 424). At last, he joins the ranks of men like Daniel Corvo as he sadly states, "Podían habernos salvado los muchachos. Ya ve usted, y sin embargo" (p. 464). Thus even sincere dedication and an unselfish purpose in life are eventually to be crushed. Whether it is a belief in the dignity of man (Diego Herrera), a wish to better humanity (Daniel Corvo), or simply a desire to love and be loved (Isabel Corvo), man's fate is to be continually frustrated in his attempts to realize his goals.

The characteristics of the adult world, the relationship of the individual with reality, and notably his sense of estrangement from life, offer interesting parallels with French existentialist literature, especially the conditions of the absurd as set forth by Camus. His philosophy of the absurd, particularly the manner in which a sense of the absurd may arise, coincides with the attitude of a character such as Daniel Corvo: "Dans un univers soudain privé d'illusions et de lumières, l'homme se sent un étranger. Cet exil est sans recours puis-qu'il est privé des souvenirs d'une patrie perdue ou de l'espoir d'une terre promise. Ce divorce entre l'homme et sa vie . . . c'est proprement le sentiment de l'absurdité."[6] Daniel's own position, brought on by the triumph of an unacceptable real-ity over his ideals, also reflects another of Camus's conditions: "Le sentiment de l'absurdité ne naît pas du simple examen d'un fait ou d'une impression mais qu'il jaillit de la comparai-son entre un état de fait et une certaine realité, entre une action et le monde qui la dépasse. L'absurde est essentielle-ment un divorce."[7]

The angle from which the character views existence also reflects his feeling of the absurd. Matute's harmonization of style with the mood of the character is very evident in this respect: metaphoric constructions transmit to the reader the adult's impression of a strange, alien world. A pictorial em-phasis, representing the dissonance between the character and reality, transmits Daniel's imprecise relationship with past and present. One example of this is the use of eyes as a point of comparison: "El espejillo cuadrado, barato, salpicado de negro, como hollín, brillando lívidamente. Parecía un ojo triste y antiguo, clavado en la pared" (Los hijos muertos, p. 287).[8] The author carries the process of humanization one step further: she qualifies the object with an adjective which disconnects it even more from reality (the mirror as un ojo triste y antiguo). This is merely the adult's impression of absurdity transmitted through the objects that surround him.

Los hijos muertos offers the outstanding study of adulthood in Matute's work, for Daniel's life is traced with a thorough-ness lacking in the other novels. Furthermore, the other adults who complement his attitudes or undergo a similar process of disillusionment, reflect or emphasize the inevitable fate of man. Other works also introduce adult characters, but as a rule Matute does not present them in such a methodical manner. They have generally reached adulthood when the story begins, thus sparing the reader the sad trajectory from idealism to discouragement. They are full-fledged adults, frozen in the characteristic positions of their age, and adopt for the most part the attitudes of their archetype Daniel Corvo, or at the very least, reinforce certain aspects of the adult mentality typified by Daniel.

La trampa also has a large collection of adults, although not all receive as extensive treatment as those of *Los hijos muertos*. Matia, Borja, Mario, and Isa represent the younger generation of adults; also treated are their parents (Emilia, Franc, Beverly) and the grandmother. Each interprets reality through his unhappy experiences, contributing some aspect of despair to the total picture of disillusionment. Most coincide in their sense of failure, frustration, dissatisfaction, loneliness, or indifference.

Matia's solitude is marked by the usual inability to communicate with either the younger generation (symbolized by Bear) or the older adults. Even her understanding with Mario is born of mutual suffering and an acknowledgment of negative characteristics common to both: doubt, treachery, and disillusionment.

Matia's indifference recalls Daniel's apathetic stage of life which followed the complete collapse of hope. Her definition of her fortieth birthday reflects this: "uno de esos crueles y útiles relojes que fabricamos pacientemente, para explicarnos el porqué nos invaden la indiferencia, el desamor, las irreparables ausencias" (*La trampa,* p. 84). Also, like Daniel, Matia escapes through her self-imposed apathy, her studied indifference. Mario adds another adult facet in his description of Matia's return to the past: "Desde la cima de su presente, tan dolientemente adquirido, año tras año, corre desesperadamente hacia atrás, busca algún cabo suelto que seguramente debe balancearse en vacío; para asirse a él, tal vez, y remontarse hacia un país o una razón más convincentes que este suelo y esta razón" (p. 183).

Matia is aware of events, but prefers commentary to action, realizing the hopelessness of intervening in affairs that already bear the aura of predestination.[9] Even an acknowledgment of the absurdity of the world stirs no desire to rebel: "Esta madrugada experimento la decepcionante sensación de que el mundo existe, simplemente; de que rueda, inane, sin clave alguna; cumpliendo sus ciclos con el deshumanizado placer que provoca, por ejemplo, el bostezo de algún dios" (pp. 25–26). Her recognition of the hopeless state of man— "Ya no hay héroes" (p. 180)—sounds strangely like one of Daniel's speeches, and looking to her past, she can see the distance between her ideals and reality: "Nadie tenía la culpa sino yo . . . que había creído infinidad de frases, que había leído, y creído, que el mundo estaba repleto de bondad" (p. 229). Other remarks comment ironically on her own credulity in once believing the myth of the "happy ending."

Mario shares many of the characteristics which are obviously reflections of an archetypal pattern after which most of Matute's adults are modeled. He too has an obsession with the past, dredging up unhappy memories which he cannot dispel. Even now he is haunted by the same feelings and desire to escape as the other adults: "Todos mis actos se reducen a una huida pavorosa; porque lo que de verdad me empujó y me arrojó fue el espanto" (p. 59). Still other signs which connect him with Matute's view of adulthood are his radical alienation and his feeling of not belonging; his refusal to become involved in more than superficial relationships— "No es agradable el conocimiento del ser humano. No es bueno llevar a extremos-límite el amor" (p. 62)—and his self-disgust as he admits his qualities as a *mercader*.

Borja is a secondary character, but he presents one of the most pitiful figures. He is still waiting for his grandmother to die and leave him her money, the only fact which gives purpose to his life. Instead of the indifference of his cousin Matia, he prefers the farce of acting out old, meaningless forms: the gracious way of life, class pretensions, and so forth. Beyond this, he seems to have no substance.

Isa's bitter outlook reflects the self-interest, egoism, and pettiness of others. Her fiancé has jilted her, preferring to marry into a more moneyed family. Her preoccupation now is to keep Mario with her, since she realizes that he is about to abandon her. Hers is an active grief—much like that of Isabel Corvo and her feelings toward Daniel—and like Isabel, her whole life is devoted to trying to retain Mario, blindly refusing to admit failure, even in the face of certain defeat.

Further exploration of the outstanding characteristics of adulthood provides new insights into Matute's view of life. Most of her adults share feelings which are far from optimistic, and, like Daniel, all move slowly toward disillusionment. A brief analysis of their most important traits reveals a surprising similarity in outlook.

Admissions of the brutality and horror of life characterize the protagonists' outlook. Marco endows his departure from Oiquixa with symbolic grandeur by saying, "Yo me llevo el rencor, la maldad, el egoísmo, la dureza de corazón de Kale Nagusia. Yo me llevo la vanidad, la estupidez, la falsa seguridad" (*Pequeño teatro*, p. 256). *Historias de la Artámila* studies in somber tones the selfish and uncharitable side of man: people refuse to give work to an old man and his grandson, then stone them when they are forced to steal in order to eat ("Los alambradores"); townspeople stone an honest miner when he returns from a prison sentence, even though all know of his heroism in a train wreck ("El mundelo"). Hypocrisy is aptly portrayed in "Los de la tienda" (*El arrepentido*), in which an "honest" storekeeper gives his godson counterfeit money. A vivid picture of cruelty and pitilessness characterizes these people, as well: a doctor refuses to save a dying man until the poverty-stricken family can pay him an outstanding bill ("La chusma").[10]

Constant disappointments and the frustration of his goals create the defeated attitude of the protagonist. Juan Medinao's failure to keep Pablo in Artámila embitters him; he finally admits that his half-brother will always be "fuera de su alma y de su cuerpo, más allá de su sangre y de su espíritu. Él [Juan] era un hombre condenado al vacío, a la ausencia" (*Fiesta al noroeste*, p. 125). The schoolmaster of "El maestro" (*El arrepentido*) acknowledges the futility of his dreams as he recalls his slow transformation from idealism to indifference. His failure to shatter the apathy of the townspeople has slowly broken him: "Creía que había venido al mundo para la abnegación y la eficacia, por ejemplo. Para redimir alguna cosa, acaso. Para defender alguna causa perdida, quizá" (p. 146). Comparing his youthful outlook with his present bitterness, the schoolmaster recalls the first days spent in the town: "Llegué aquí creyendo encontrar niños: sólo había larvas de hombres, malignas larvas, cansadas y desengañadas antes del uso de razón" (p. 147). He repudiates mankind in the same way as Daniel or Pablo: "Antes, fue un exaltado defensor de los hombres. . . . Acaso, de hombres como él mismo ahora. Pero no, él no se reconocía ninguna dignidad" (p. 147). Their solitude, too, follows the same patterns. Kepa, the unhappy father of Zazu, "no veía nada que no fuera su propio corazón, porque estaba profundamente solo" (*Pequeño teatro*, p. 14); he later asks "¿Por qué es la vida tan hueca, tan vacía?" (p. 203). Even in the middle of the revolution, Pablo Barral feels this remoteness: "En el minuto de la victoria estaba solo, en el vacío, como una estrella que cae, que siempre cae, sin lograr el destino" (*En esta tierra*, p. 199).

Matute's other adult protagonists share Daniel's desire to escape, for although they do not use his words, their actions point to a rejection of life through escape, a symbolic self-destruction, or suicide.[11] Kepa continually drinks because "Ahora, quería escapar a la realidad. 'Esta vida vacía, cochina vida, asco' " (*Pequeño teatro*, p. 81); Marco's invitation to Ilé is founded on the same principle: "Abandona a estos hombres, a estos pobres hombres sucios y avaros, a estos hombres de alma turbia y egoísta, y sígueme" (*Pequeño teatro*, p. 136). Pablo, of *En esta tierra*, also drinks to escape from "aquel mundo lento y asfixiante, primitivo y monótono, embotado, sin ayer ni mañana, sin tiempo."[12]

Old age, the unhappy conclusion of adulthood, also has its representatives in Matute's works, although none is as developed as the younger adults. Her old people suffer from loneliness in a more personal, pathetic way. Their tragedies do not stem from social or ideological causes, as in characters like Daniel or Pablo, but from neglect, disrespect, uselessness. One of the most touching examples of this is "Vida nueva," in which two old men meet on New Year's day and speak in glowing terms of their full, happy lives. Each goes home— one to the family who has moved him to the attic and denies him even the joy of playing with his own grandchildren; the other to his boarding house where he writes a New Year's card saying "No estás solo, querido amigo, aunque todos han muerto. Felicidades," and mails it to himself (*El tiempo*, p. 232). Further cases of thoughtless neglect or inconsiderateness occur in "La isla," in which an old nurse is put into a home for the aged because she can no longer do the expected work, and in "Los niños buenos," where the grandfather wants only to be loved by his dogs and respected by the townspeople and never realizes either wish.

Many of the old people embody a state of degeneration. Gerardo Corvo exemplifies both mental and physical deterioration in this group: he is indifferent to his surroundings, neglectful of his personal appearance; his heavy drinking and unconcern with his life are other signs of this apathy. These adults may acknowledge a disgust with the pettiness of life: "Sólo quedaba un mundo imbécil y cobarde, sórdido, de trabajo y de comida grosera, de vino malo . . . de maldad pequeña, sin grandeza y sin locura" (*Los hijos muertos*, pp. 259–60); and their disgust may culminate in a desire to die (Gerardo Corvo envies the luck of the guard who has just been buried) or to be spared the necessity of living: "El viejo Barral deseó ser tan pequeño, tan indiferente a la vida de los hombres como aquel insecto pegado a un muro, ajeno al mundo, absorto en su egoísta insignificancia" (*En esta tierra*, p. 166). In fact, Barral has been rejecting life from the time he was a young man, for he prefers the refuge found in study to an active interest in his family.

The only old women who are presented in any detail are the grandmothers in *En esta tierra*, *Primera memoria* and *La trampa*. The similarity between these three characters, and the duplication of some of their salient characteristics in others (the grandmother in "La oveja negra," for example), suggest that Matute has used a living person for a model. These women are hard, self-centered, and hypocritical, especially in matters of religion. The loneliness and sadness of their male contemporaries does not affect them: unloving and unloved, they are completely indifferent to anything that does not bear directly on themselves.

Providing a living background for the main actors in these novels are groups of characters which reappear throughout Matute's works: the lower classes, servants, doctors, and rural school teachers. Most are obviously generalized because their mission as representatives of a group outweighs their individuality. Many of these minor figures remain nameless, adding a pathetic anonymity to their already unhappy lives: a character in the story "El hijo" (*El arrepentido*) is referred to only as *Ésa*; in "El hermoso amanecer," there are people such as *la Madre, la Mujer,* and several nameless *hombres.* Matute has confirmed that many of these secondary characters have their counterparts in real life.[13] The use of living models may also account for the characteristics which keep reappearing in people of the same class or profession.

"Los de abajo," as they are called by Daniel in *Los hijos muertos,* loom large in Matute's works: they are either represented by a single person—la Tanaya, for example—or presented as an inseparable mass forming a living background (*Los Abel, Fiesta al noroeste, Los hijos muertos, Historias de la Artámila,* to mention only a few), and they are a constant preoccupation of the author. The description of these peasants reveals the dire misery in which they live. The brief resumé of the life of an *hombre de aldea* given by Eloy in *Los Abel* is typical of Matute's expositional powers in treating these people,[14] for throughout the description one glimpses their latent hopelessness, their animallike attitude, both in violence and in stoic acceptance, and their heedlessness concerning the future.[15] Valba Abel's description of the men of her town is also indicative of the state in which these people live: "En aquel pueblo nuestro trabajaban hombres y brutos abrazados a un mismo suelo, mezclado su sudor. Ni una máquina, ni un descanso, ni una dulzura. . . . Bebían, bebían: todo lo apagaban en el chorro amoratado de la bota. Su suciedad era turbia como su ambición, como su desesperanza" (*Los Abel,* p. 59).

Although doctors and schoolmasters are of a higher class, their fate is even more appalling when one considers that they, at least, had the means to rise above the level of their surroundings. However, with the same undercurrent of determinism which affects the heroes of the novels, the sordid atmosphere seems to cast a spell over these people and drag them down to hopelessness with the rest. In one of her interviews, the author stated that the schoolmaster from "Los niños buenos" had a living model: "Había entonces en España muchos de aquellos maestros que llegaban al pueblo con buena fe y acababan embruteciéndose, emborrachándose, perdiendo la vida triste y sordamente."[16] In effect, the schoolmaster of this story is multiplied many times: he appears as the teachers in "El incendio" and "El río" (both in *Historias de la Artámila*), and as Pablo Barral (*En esta tierra*). Doctors also may share these characteristics (Eloy of *Los Abel*, for example).

Throughout Ana María Matute's exposition of adult life—of the individual or of the group—the keynote is pessimism. The signs which lead to this final attitude are apparent in Matute's treatment of the earlier periods of life: the clash between fantasy and reality in childhood and the disillusionment of adolescence are both preparatory experiences for the greatest failure of all: the complete failure of the adult to adjust himself to life. This failure leads to hopelessness and solitude from which the impossibility of escape can only be described as fatalistic. The life cycle closes not with death, but with a disillusionment that casts an aura of futility on man's existence. Matute offers neither direct comments nor solutions; her eloquent silence is enough.

5. Style and Artistic Vision

Realism of situation in Ana María Matute's works is the point of departure for her analysis of the characters, whom she portrays from within, creating a psychological reality in which introspection may distort exterior reality. Thus action in these novels might better be defined as reaction, for the protagonists are continually forced to adjust or redefine their goals. This character-oriented approach has the advantage of controlling the sympathies of the reader, who, deprived of an omniscient vision, can view the world only through the eyes of the characters. Certain important stylistic devices reinforce the characters' mental vision and certain techniques tend to be associated with specific character types and themes; thus, the seemingly contradictory terms used by critics to describe her style—poetic, direct, starkly realistic, epic, crude, delicate, chaotic—are all equally valid, depending on the work in question.

Several consistent elements bear discussion because they show so clearly Matute's use of technique as a means of oblique communication with the reader, through emphasis on themes or character outlook. For this reason, I shall present an analysis of only the outstanding techniques in her literature, of those which appear regularly and which she obviously feels have the most impact, for she works and reworks them, using them to highlight themes or character viewpoint, to criticize or praise, to create the necessary ambiance or to capture the reader's sympathies. The major features of her style are rhetorical devices (especially repetition, accumulation, and recurrent phrases or symbols); variations on literary archetypes; realism of specific minor characters; pathetic fallacy and nature imagery; and colors used with symbolic import.

Several rhetorical devices stand out as obvious means of distorting reality; repetition is an artistic resort common to almost every work by Matute. Repetition of words, phrases, or word patterns has a decidedly auditory appeal, and the author is skillful in her use of prose rhythms, as in the parallel, tripartite structure which often appears: "Esto no lo sabía Kepa de una manera concreta, pero lo adivinaba en las miradas rápidas e intensas de su hija, en sus frases secas y breves, en sus risas intempestivas y agudas" (*Pequeño teatro*, p. 106).

She often repeats a single word or phrase for its lyrical or rhythmic effect: "Poco tiempo después, se enroló en un buque mercante y huyó mar adentro, mar negro y rojo, mar de mil colores, menos azul, menos verde" (*Pequeño teatro*, p. 17). This same repetition, expanded, frequently links longer grammatical units, usually punctuated as fragmentary sentences. The incomplete phrases create loose associations which suggest rather than express an idea. In the following quotation, the recurrence of *polvos* and *cajas* merges the fragmentary sentences into a long, dramatic period which produces a coherent impression: "La admiración que sentían las muchachas de Kale Nagusia por Zazu, era una admiración avergonzada y oculta, como se ocultaban los granillos de la pubertad tras los polvos blancos y olorosos. Aquellos polvos con que la madre les permitía cubrir las naricillas brillantes. Los polvos de las inefables cajas azul y violeta, con un primoroso lazo pintado en la tapa. Las enternecedoras cajas de polvos que se vendían en la 'Gran Droguería de Arresu Hermanos' " (*Pequeño teatro*, p. 34). *Los hijos muertos* also uses the single recurring word to link paragraphs that shuttle between present and past, using italics to distinguish the two time periods visually:

> La muñeca de la Tanaya. Qué absurdo, a estas alturas, el recuerdo de la muñeca le dolía, a él.
>
> *La vio por vez primera, como escondiendo muchas*

*cosas en su corazón de palo. Igual a la muñeca de la
madre, igual a la muñeca de la abuela. . . . La muñeca
consistía en dos ramitas en cruz, atadas y envueltas en un
jirón de falda.*

Aquella muñeca, a él, le traía el recuerdo de la niña
de la Tanaya. Y a la niña de la Tanaya tampoco, de ninguna manera, la quería recordar.

*Por ella fue, por la niña de la Tanaya, quizá, que em-
pezó él a odiar de un modo concreto. . . .* (p. 62)

Retrospection plays a great part in these novels; and the
leitmotif—a further refinement of repetition—complements
retrospection with its double function of poetic association
and ironic contrast. The leitmotif, a phrase connected with a
person or an idea, appears at irregular intervals, recalling
former dreams or ideas, and contrasting them with the present. *Pequeño teatro* associates this technique with the main
characters. When reminded of his poor, wretched daughter,
Kepa thinks, "Hemos logrado una juventud perfecta," unaware of the irony of his statement. He repeats this phrase
verbatim at times when Zazu is obviously disturbed, perhaps
as a means of convincing himself that all is well (pp. 20,
196); he sees a marionette who reminds him of his daughter
and unconsciously repeats the same words, further establish-
ing the parallel between marionettes and characters (p. 97).
Neither this phrase nor the other motifs are overworked; they
appear where they can most enrich the situation. Zazu's
theme ("Mi corazón y yo crecimos extrañamente") comes up
only in connection with her self-analysis and admission of
unhappiness.

Los hijos muertos continually interweaves past with present, emphasizing the characters' present disillusionment by
recalling former happiness. The principal characters are unable to divorce the past from the present, and the novelist
conveys their mental state to the reader by using the leitmotif,

piling up associations which are reintroduced each time the theme is repeated. White flowers which emit an overwhelming perfume recall La Encrucijada, home of the Corvo family. They are a symbol of decadence, and as such evoke class differences and Daniel's alienation: "En aquel Hegroz que odiaba silenciosamente, orgullosamente, La Encrucijada. Sabía Daniel que si alguno pasaba cerca de ella camino del trabajo, de los pagos, el olor denso de la flor blanca, el olor terrible y sofocante de la flor blanca, bajo las grandes estrellas del verano, reverdecía el odio" (p. 53). Isabel's desire to restore her home to its former glory haunts her with the words "Hay que levantar La Encrucijada." Daniel's two leitmotifs (his *cuerda de alianza* and *tiempo de esperanza*) originate in his youthful solidarity with the lower classes. Although these phrases are repeated throughout his early adventures, they provide a most effective contrast to his hopeless situation after his defeat.

Pablo, the unhappy revolutionary of *En esta tierra*, also has two such phrases associated with his life: one, a memory of the happy childhood days when he and his father collected insects: "Mariposas clavadas, escarabajos negros, alas de color de plata" (p. 226); the second phrase, also the epigraph, comes from Deuteronomy: "Verás de frente la tierra que yo daré a los hijos de Israel: Y no entrarás en ella." The intuition that he will never cross over his Jordan haunts Pablo to the moment of his death.

In all cases, the leitmotif provides ironic contrast between the present and the past, maintaining the constant tension through continual references to a more attractive past or a vanished idealism. In *Primera memoria*, symbols of childhood serve a similar purpose. Matia's bitter knowledge of the certain loss of her childhood alternates with parenthetical comments evoking a happier past, or despairing exclamations at her present wretched state. Poetic evocation through description or parenthetical commentary enables the reader to associate the adolescent's state of mind with her present situation. Thus the constant references to fairy-tale characters, juxtaposed with the discovery of cruelty, sex, and hatred, reflect Matia's wish to return to the safety of childhood; the remembrance of her kind old nurse is most significant in the light of her antipathy toward her grandmother. References to a book of Andersen's fairy tales, especially to "The Little Mermaid," and to Peter Pan (both concerned with eternal youth and innocence) parallel the bitter realization that there is no way back to childhood: "(No existió la Isla de Nunca Jamás y la Joven Sirena no consiguió un alma inmortal, porque los hombres y las mujeres no aman, y se quedó con un par de inútiles piernas, y se convirtió en espuma.) Eran horribles los cuentos" (p. 243).

Several stores in *El tiempo* use symbols in much the same way; once established, the symbol always evokes the same emotions and meaning without lengthy background information. The train in "El tiempo" represents time; the horrible overhead lamp of "La ronda" serves a similar purpose. References to these two symbols appear at strategic moments, reminding both the reader and protagonist of the passage of time: "Se iba uno a la vejez sin sentirlo, sin saberlo, sin edad concreta. Sin remedio. Y no había ningún día fijo en que empezara la vejez. Esto era lo insoportable. De nuevo sintió como si la lámpara de allí en su casa temblara sobre su cabeza" (pp. 96–97).

Repetition of associated themes provides an effortless transition between memory and actuality in *Los hijos muertos*; it provides a poetic overlay in *Pequeño teatro*, the lyrical rhythms enhancing the distortion of reality. Such rhetorical devices, however, serve a double function in Ana María Matute's works; they are purely artistic devices in the above examples; in other cases they tend to be linked with criticism of undesirable conditions.

The note of protest evident in *Pequeño teatro* has grown steadily stronger in later works, the nonconformity showing clearly in the special stylistic devices which, in an emotion-charged way, transmit the author's ideas to the reader. Matute has been aware of a sense of injustice in life since an early age; her preface to an American edition of *Historias de la Artámila* speaks of a childhood episode which greatly affected her outlook: "Podría decir que mi vocación de escritora nace del hecho—auténtico—relatado en este libro bajo el título de 'Los chicos.' Aquel sentimiento, mezcla de dolor, rebeldía y arrepentimiento, que me brotara por primera vez ante un hecho injusto y cruel, fue, digo yo, la 'levadura,' la raíz más profunda de mi vocación de escritora. Y todo el libro es una continuación de aquello que fueron viviendo y observando mis diez años, ante un mundo desconocido y a menudo incomprensible."[1] This realization of the division between the privileged and the underprivileged appears throughout her works, for she feels strongly about the mission of literature: "A la par que un documento de nuestro tiempo y un planteamiento de los problemas del hombre actual, [la novela] debe herir . . . la conciencia de la sociedad, en un deseo de mejorarla."[2] The specifically social function of the novel and the commitment of the writer to this function appear in a later interview: "El escritor se halla comprometido, ante todo, con la verdad; con la verdad enfrentada a la problemática del tiempo que le ha tocado vivir. Y no debe aceptar consignas."[3] Matute investigates problems of a social or ethical nature; each problem is associated with definite rhetorical devices.

Social criticism is most evident in her lengthy descriptions of the miserable conditions of the lower classes: their unhappy lives, their poverty, and their sense of deprivation. Her style and technique lend themselves well to this kind of commentary: the author chronicles the lives of these people most graphically, selecting those details of a sordid existence which harmonize with the main character's unhappy state.

Accumulative description generally accompanies the exposition of some social evil, as if the profusion of nouns somehow should suggest the weight of one's misery: "Hombres y mujeres, niños, amontonados en torno a patinillos interiores, como en covachas de murciélagos, arracimados en la oscuridad como murciélagos, nocturnos y viscosos. Con sus sudores, sus sueños, sus pus, sus toses, sus gargajos, su pan, sus costras de mugre, sus guisos grasientos . . . sus riñas, sus partos, su cansancio, su desilusión, sus sueños, sus pantalones deshilachados, sus zapatos agrietados, sus peines pringosos, llenos de mechones y de una extraña roña" (*Los hijos muertos*, pp. 125–26). Accumulation and repetition for critical purposes are especially prevalent in *En esta tierra* and *Los hijos muertos*; both are novels in which the protagonists fight to better these conditions, and fail. The following passage is typical of many describing the women of the lower classes, a subject to which the author returns time and again: "Las mujeres gastadas, enflaquecidas, resecas, de belleza perdida, de juventud perdida, de vida perdida. Su odio era el más violento y ensañado, el que no perdonaba. Sin fondo, como su amargura. Trabajaban como bestias desde niñas, y parían hijos flacos, hambrientos, bajo el sol implacable, el cielo implacable, el polvo implacable" (*En esta tierra*, p. 187).

Through the tumultuous impact of such misery, the reader can sense the novelist's sympathy. She uses nature to form a metaphoric protest in the extremely intricate sentence which follows: "Tuvieron que ir ellos tirando del arado (en la mañana aquella de septiembre, con un cielo bajo y gris contra la tierra encarnada: aquella pieza de tierra donde saltaban los pedruscos blancos y manchados de barro, como cráneos de un cementerio diminuto), el hermano y la hermana Migueles, de dieciséis y catorce años, huérfanos de jornaleros de Lucas Enríquez, con el hombro hendido por la soga, arrastrando el arado, sin ira, con la cara sumida de la pobreza indiferente, acostumbrada, descalzos encima de la humedad grasienta del suelo, donde las piedras saltaban como dientes iracundos, rabiosos. . . . El río allí al lado fluía lentamente, indiferente como la pobreza, rodando como la miseria" (*Los hijos muertos*, p. 67). This excellent example of artistic deformation comes from another experience in the author's life.[4]

A second type of criticism deals with ethical problems, for Matute is describing the constants of human nature: hypocrisy and selfishness. Amplification condemns the town gossips in *Pequeño teatro* by magnifying an insignificant event out of proportion: "Desde hacía tiempo [Zazu] era considerada por las gentes de Kale Nagusia como 'el escándalo constante de Oiquixa.' Zazu, en la lengua de todas las viejas solteronas, de las viudas y las huérfanas de los pilotos, en las lenguas ácidas del práctico del puerto y el delgado de la Aduana, en las espesas lenguas de los tenderos y los almacenistas, en cuyos ojos sorprendía una lujuria retenida y reprobativa. Zazu, en la envidia y la curiosidad de las muchachas vírgenes y castas, en la maligna y escandalizada mirada de las hijas del capitán y del intendente" (p. 29).[5] Her most bitter attack to date has been directed against the hypocritical person who unscrupulously takes advantages of others for his own profit. These are the *mercaderes*, a collective word which refers to all unprincipled people and which also serves as the title for her trilogy. Accumulative description reinforces the criticism of these profiteers: "(Mercaderes por todas parte. . . . Lógicos, sólidos, naturales mercaderes. . . . Todos, sentados pacientemente a la puerta de su tienda, esperando. Esperándome. Abanicándose el sudor, y esperándome. Gordos, sabios, útiles mercaderes. A la puerta de las guerras, a la puerta del hambre, del deseo, abanicándose, sonriendo, esperando. La vida es eso: un rechoncho y paciente mercader, sentado a la puerta de su tienda, de su puesto, de su cuchitril: esperando, con un brillo contenido y ácido en los ojillos. . . .)" (p. 75).

Also under attack is the false Christian who uses religion to mask his own selfish motives. Biblical motifs and religious allusions highlight the actions of such protagonists. Juan Medinao, who hypocritically uses religion as an easy escape from the responsibilities of life, is made ridiculous by ironic religious metaphors. He meets Dingo "Abrazándole como una cruz de plomo" (p. 26); he associates Dingo and the stolen money with Judas and the thirty pieces of silver. Isabel Corvo (*Los hijos muertos*) is another case in point: she assiduously attends mass but refuses to improve the wretched conditions of the poor. *Primera memoria* is fraught with religious symbolism, from the name Manuel to the cock crowing after Matia's betrayal of her friend; *Los soldados lloran de noche* continues the same themes. *El arrepentido* makes extensive use of religious material ("Mañana," "El hijo," "El embustero"); "Yo no he venido a traer la paz . . ."[6] attacks the *mercaderes'* perversion of Christian charity with a parablelike development of several Biblical passages. Biblical quotations and the modernization of Biblical characters also help to comment on this apparently eternal, unchanging aspect of human nature.[7]

Religious material which reinforces criticism or comments on the nature of man also appears in Matute's characterization. She reworks the character of several literary archetypes of Biblical origin, notably Cain and Abel. *Fiesta al noroeste*, for example, is one of many novels containing new interpretations of the figures of Cain and Abel. Matute's fascination with the Biblical pair and the artistic liberties she has taken with the subject have drawn the attention of several critics[8]; she has often mentioned her constant interest in the theme: "Ese amor oscuro que le empuja [a Juan], ese deseo de 'beber' y 'devorar' la pureza del hermano despojado de todo, es una constante del odio entre hermanos que desde *Los Abel* ha sido para mí otro tema predilecto."[9] In her reinterpretation of the Biblical motif, she establishes a pattern which involves some stylization: the description of two men—at times, although not always, related—with entirely different natures. One feels strangely drawn to the other and tries to conquer or destroy him. Although the Abel of *Fiesta al noroeste* (Pablo) can get along very well without Cain (Juan Medinao), the latter desperately needs the former. The deformation of Juan's character is, in effect, the transference of all the usual love for life and freedom to Pablo, leaving Juan an incomplete person. Juan Medinao feels attracted to his half-brother because the latter fills some need in Juan's personality: "Ahora comprendía que Pablo era parte de sí mismo. Él no era como el molde hueco de su hermano, y lo necesitaba, deseaba su contenido más allá de toda razón" (p. 111). The use of the confessional as a narrative device and the constant references to religion provide a good background for Juan Medinao's state of mind (a religious preoccupation which is sterile, which emphasizes not life, but death). The stylization of his character is an intentional deformation of personality to illustrate the Cain-Abel theme.

The problem of the static character is more understandable in this light, for the figure of "Abel"—that is, the person who is untroubled by mental anguish, who unquestioningly accepts what life has to offer—appears throughout these works. He is Tito in *Los Abel*, Pablo in *Fiesta al noroeste*, Manuel in *Primera memoria* and *Los soldados lloran de noche*, Miguel in "La ronda" (*El tiempo*), Marcial in "Los hermanos" (*El río*), the brother in "Noticia del joven K" (*Algunos muchachos*), and to a certain extent Cristián (*En esta tierra*). These Abels are the missing part of Cain's personality, giving rise to the love-hate attraction that the novelist associates with the Biblical pair.

This analysis may be applied to *Los hijos muertos*, in which the unhappy Daniel is pitted against two people who represent qualities which he has long since abandoned: Isabel's efficiency contrasts with Daniel's lassitude; Diego Herrera's idealism is a foil for his friend's disillusionment. This novel also suggests a broader interpretation of the Cain and Abel theme: contrasting personalities within the family, in which the desire to love, possess, and destroy form a single purpose, create complex and dramatic human relationships.

In two similar works (*Los Abel* and "La ronda") Cain kills Abel; "Los hermanos" and "Noticia del joven K" retell essentially the same story; in *Fiesta al noroeste*, Juan symbolically conquers his Abel by raping the latter's mother; and Borja treacherously rids himself of his Abel (Manuel) by having him unjustly sent to reform school (*Primera memoria*). The family ties that bind Pablo and Cristián in *En esta tierra* fall into the same category: "El amor amargo y difícil, oscuro de los hombres, en lucha constante y desesperada" (p. 222). Further analogies may be drawn on a wider scale: the Civil War, the "lucha entre hermanos,"[10] is treated extensively in both *En esta tierra* and *Los hijos muertos*, and echoed on a smaller scale in *Primera memoria*.

Although Cain and Abel are the most popular archetypes, Matute uses others drawn from Biblical sources. Moses is the model for Pablo (*En esta tierra*), established by the title and quotations from Deuteronomy. More oblique references in *Primera memoria* and *Los soldados lloran de noche* evoke the Christ-figure. In the former, the actions of Borja and Matia repeat on a small scale the betrayal of Jesus; in *Los soldados lloran de noche*, Manuel and Jeza (a possible allusion to the name of Jesus) sustain parallels with Christ (the idea of self-sacrifice, redemption, washing away the sins of the world). In all these cases, the literary archetype adds to the sense of fatality. Once the reader becomes aware of the analogy, he is also aware of the character's irrevocable fate. Pablo, like Moses, will never reach the Promised Land; Cain must destroy Abel; Christ must be betrayed and sacrificed.

In sections of previous chapters, I have concentrated on the vision of the main protagonists which creates a stylized picture of the secondary characters. In *Primera memoria*, Matia's dislike of her grandmother, for example, transforms the old lady into a horrible creature whose constant prying causes Matia to use eyes—the means of this prying—as the basis for her unfavorable portrait: she describes the grandmother's eyes as "dos peces tentaculares" (p. 202), "dos hormigas" (p. 210), "ojos de lechuza" (p. 238). This strange vision must be understood in the light of Matia's reaction to her grandmother who, with her aunt Emilia, stands for all the horror of growing up. Matia projects her own emotions onto the grandmother's person, for the description comes from within the protagonist, validating the expressionistic manner of narration.

On the other hand, there is a group of minor characters who escape the distorting focus of the protagonist's eye. The author describes them directly, realistically, and with an uncommon concision. Two such sketches occur in *Los hijos muertos*. La Tanaya, Matute states, was taken from living models: "La dureza de aquella tierra [Castilla], el caciquismo, la paciencia resignada de los campesinos han dejado gran huella en mí. Sobre esta paciencia sólo comparable a la de la tierra, especialmente la de sus mujeres, he hablado en *Los hijos muertos*. La figura de la Tanaya está sacada de la realidad de varias mujeres de aquel país—por eso la quiero."[11] La Tanaya appears in brief sketches: as a child, when she would peek into the windows of the house, as a young girl baking bread, as a woman who has a child out of wedlock, and finally as a married woman, old and resigned: "Sí—dijo ella—. Tuve muchos hijos. . . . Y alguno se me murió. . . . Luego, vinieron otros. . . . Y aún pueden llegar más. Así es la vida" (p. 557).

El Patinito is another example of a portrait in miniature. He spends long hours discussing life with Daniel, and is one of the greatest influences in the boy's life. From a series of flashbacks we learn that he was the child of a prostitute who loved and cared for him tenderly; after years of hard work and study he became a schoolmaster and was sent to Hegroz. The brief but pithy description makes him one of the most human, touching characters in the book.

There are even shorter sketches, dealing mainly with people from the lower classes. With the briefest details, these characters come alive through the pen of the artist. Such vignettes show Matute's realism most strongly, providing descriptions of people, places, and scenes from daily life. The funeral vigil in *Fiesta al noroeste,* where the peasants serve coffee and put paper flowers in the dead child's mouth, the quick impression of a farmyard with a woman calling chickens to feed them (*Los Abel*), the picture of Tanaya on the day she bakes, are but a few of these realistic descriptions. *Historias de la Artámila* and *El río* use this technique most consistently, doubtless because most of the material is drawn from real life. Proof of this may be seen in the preface to *Historias de la Artámila* and in an interview in which Matute describes some experiences which she transfers to her work.[12]

The sparse imagery throughout *Historias de la Artámila* draws almost exclusively on nature, reinforcing the important relationship between the people and the land. The use of local color also adds a realistic, almost *costumbrista* effect to the narrative: An old man regularly lets a bee sting him whenever he has rheumatism, saying, "Ahora el reuma se va a hacer gárgaras" (p. 83). The city children receive a strange lesson in botany from one of the local boys: "—De ésta, si mordéis, moriréis con la fiebre metida en el estómago, como una piedra. . . . —De ésta, si la ponéis bajo la almohada, no despertaréis. . . . —De ésta, el primo Jacinto murió a la madrugada, por haberla olido con los pies descalzos" (p. 37).

Nature has a unique function in Ana María Matute's works. A cleverly planned background reinforces the pervading atmosphere of tension (seen in the yearning for an unattainable childhood innocence or in a conflict between two people or, especially, within the protagonist, such as Matia). The background is a living, threatening, and integral part of the work, both harmonizing with and translating the protagonist's state of mind through pathetic fallacy and other nature imagery. Man's solitude is reinforced by a menacing natural world, indifferent to his suffering, at times deformed to give new dimensions to the violence of emotions or events. For example, in *Fiesta al noroeste,* when Dingo returns to Artámila, the barren land which he so hates, his feelings are transferred to natural phenomena, and the sky and land are described as hostile to man (p. 9); the malevolence of nature stands out in such phrases as "un camino precipitado y violento, hecho sólo para tragar" (p. 10), "sus cielos implacables" (p. 11), "La lluvia . . . indiferente" (p. 13).[13] Likewise, *Primera memoria* abounds in a living, menacing kind of nature, found in such descriptions as "un cielo hinchado como una infección gris" (p. 23); "Una [pita] estaba rota, con los bordes resecos como una cicatriz" (p. 43); or "no eran días de tregua. El cielo parecía tapado por una nube grande, hinchada y rojiza" (p. 157). This type of description prevails as well in other novels: the Abels' house looks out on "un barranco violento y torturado" (*Los Abel,* p. 10), and nature enhances the characters' states of mind in *Los hijos muertos* with such terms as "una luna salvaje" (p. 261), "El viento . . . con sus mil gritos lejanos como voces de muertos" (p. 343), or "este mar lento y siniestro, con su lengua despaciosa y cruel avanzando y retrocediendo, igual que un gran animal goloso" (p. 418).

The sun plays the most important symbolic role of all the nature images, and because of its consistent association with violence and hostility it is the most interesting example of how nature is deformed to enhance the fatalistic elements in these works. *Primera memoria* is set under a blinding sun which simultaneously describes, foreshadows, and incites the fierce action: "El sol feroz y maligno" (p. 40); "Y el sol, allí fuera, acechando algo, como un león" (p. 108); "El sol atravesaba la piel transparente del cielo, como una hinchada quemazón" (p. 209). The adjectives in the following quotation evoke repressed violence to reinforce the symbolism of the sun: "Por encima de la cúpula de mosaicos verdes, arrancándoles un llamear dañino, estaba el sol, rojo y feroz en medio del cielo pálido. . . . Una cruel sensación de violencia, un irritado fuego ardía allá arriba: todo invadido, empapado en aquella luz negra" (p. 79). A burning sun presides over the savage battle in which Daniel participates: "El gran sol impávido tenía una risa muda y grande, chorreante de fuego" (*Los hijos muertos*, pp. 152–53); the day that Miguel escapes from the camp and kills a fellow prisoner, "El sol brillaba mucho. Brillaba de un modo insólito, reverberante, terrible" (*Los hijos muertos*, p. 393).

Although the sun takes first place among nature images, other images also accentuate the atmosphere of tension: the inversion of commonly accepted elements of nature into symbols of the grotesque disharmony of the protagonist and the world. The novelist prefers to ignore the more traditional symbols that denote violence, such as storms and roaring wind. Instead, she creates tension with elements of nature which normally evoke happier images. The flowers in *Primera memoria* are an example. Traditional symbolism equates them with transitoriness, spring, or beauty.[14] Preferring her own symbolism, Matute creates a new equation of flowers with anger: "Creí que latiría en su voz la misma ira de las flores" (p. 42).[15]

Still devising new means to maintain the intense emotional level, Matute often describes an object in antithetical terms. Oxymoron is used most strikingly with auditory effects combining sound and silence: "De pronto calló la campana y hubo un estallido de silencio" (*Primera memoria*, p. 78). She may even add synesthesia to create a more confusing image, purposely jarring the reader's sensibilities to make him empathize with Matia's troubled feelings: "El sol lucía fuera como un rojo trueno de silencio, mucho más fuerte que cualquier estampido" (p. 80).

The visual appeal of nature expands to include a gamut of colors which evoke certain moods or reinforce the special atmosphere: red, for example, has a significance analogous to that of the red flowers in *Primera memoria*. A pictorial emphasis stands out in many works, perhaps due to the author's early interest in painting.[16] "El incendio" and other pieces from *Los niños tontos* use colors as important elements. Tones are often drawn from nature; for example, the red light from the sun is frequently depicted: "el muro de piedras que tenían un resplandor rojo" (*Tres y un sueño*, p. 82). In the following description, nature becomes a painting of bright colors: "La tierra se iba oscureciendo, hasta tomar un color sangriento, y se volvían las hojas de un verde muy brillante. Algunas plantas parecían negras, otras azul oscuro. Se formaban charcos y el sol enrojecía detrás de los chopos, sobre el río" (*Tres y un sueño*, pp. 70–71). One critic has investigated the extent to which colors form an integral part of Matute's narrative, even tabulating the number of times each shade appears in the novels. As might be expected, the results show that colors have symbolic value: dark, somber tones emphasize the tragic vision.[17]

Epilogue

The reader recently acquainted with Ana María Matute's works enjoys her clever manipulation of the threads of plot, character, and style, colored with brilliant flashes of insight. Those familiar with more of her literature, however, can enjoy a better view: these threads merge into a Weltanschauung which, like a tapestry, conveys each of the autonomous creations of fiction as part of a single unit. Behind the temporal reality of the single work lie murky fixed patterns to which human behavior is subjected. To step back and look at the perspective provides interesting results indeed.

Although she treats her characters with understanding, Matute's view of man is pessimistic. Both the individual and the more universal picture of humanity reflect a hopeless position. She pits idealism against forces representing self-interest and corruption in a battle which the hero is destined to lose. Traumatic experiences move the characters from one clearly defined age to the next. The only period of innocence —childhood—is soon shattered by contact with reality, and an awareness of this reality soon leads to the disillusionment of the older characters. Cyclic-like repetition and archetypes suggest atemporal patterns of human behavior: the Cain-Abel fratricide, the sacrifice of Christ, the omnipresent *mercader* appear as prevalent today as in Biblical times.

Ana María Matute creates this literary world through the elaboration of a certain number of key themes which correspond to an overall vision of man's condition, through the use of original character types to express this conception, and through a narrative formula which uses special devices to convey this vision to the reader. The freshness of her approach, her subjective manner of expressing this unique world, and the impression of sincerity evident in all her writing, are responsible for the position of prominence she already holds in twentieth-century Spanish literature.

If Ana María Matute's view is ultimately pessimistic—the loss of childhood innocence begins the process of inevitable disillusionment—still, her compassionate treatment leaves the reader with a taste of the ambiguous triumph of generosity over self-interest and of love over hatred.

Bibliography

I. Works by Ana María Matute

A. *In Spanish*

Los Abel. Barcelona: Ediciones Destino, 1948.

Algunos muchachos. Barcelona: Ediciones Destino, 1968.

El arrepentido. Barcelona: Editorial Rocas, 1961.

"Autocrítica de *Fiesta al noroeste.*" *Correo literario* 3, no. 46 (15 April 1952): 5.

Caballito loco. Barcelona: Editorial Lumen, 1962.

Doce Historias de la Artámila. Edited by Manuel Durán and Gloria Durán. New York: Harcourt, Brace and World, 1965.

En esta tierra. Barcelona: Editorial Exito, 1955.

Fiesta al noroeste. 3d ed. Barcelona: Ediciones Destino, 1963.

Los hijos muertos. 2d ed. Barcelona: Editorial Planeta, 1960.

Historias de la Artámila. Barcelona: Ediciones Destino, 1961.

Libro de juegos para los niños de los otros. Barcelona: Editorial Lumen, 1961.

A la mitad del camino. Barcelona: Editorial Rocas, 1961.

"La mujer y la literatura." *Revista de actualidades, artes y letras* 7 (10–16 May 1958): 15.

Los niños tontos. Madrid: Ediciones Arion, 1956.

El país de la pizarra. Barcelona: Editorial Molino, 1956.

Paulina, el mundo y las estrellas. Barcelona: Editorial Garbo, 1960.

"La pequeña vida," *La novela del sábado* 1, no. 11 (n.d.): 5–64.

Pequeño teatro. 3d ed. Barcelona: Editorial Planeta, 1955.

El polizón del "Ulises." Barcelona: Editorial Lumen, 1965.

Primera memoria. Barcelona: Ediciones Destino, 1960.

El río. Barcelona: Editorial Argos, 1963.

El saltamontes verde. Barcelona: Editorial Lumen, 1960.

Los soldados lloran de noche. Barcelona: Ediciones Destino, 1964.

El tiempo. Barcelona: Editorial Mateu, 1957.
La trampa. Barcelona: Ediciones Destino, 1969.
Tres y un sueño. Barcelona: Ediciones Destino, 1961.
Untitled lecture. In *El autor enjuicia su obra,* pp. 141–51. Madrid: Editora Nacional, 1966.
"Yo no he venido a traer la paz . . . ," *Cuadernos del congreso por la libertad de la cultura,* no. 67 (December 1962), pp. 53–63.

B. English Translations of Works by Ana María Matute

Awakening [*Primera memoria*]. Translated by James Holman Mason. London: Hutchinson, 1963.
"The Foolish Children" [*Los niños tontos*]. Translated by Elaine Kerrigan. *Texas Quarterly* 4 (Spring 1961): 224–29.
The Lost Children [*Los hijos muertos*]. Translated by Joan MacLean. New York: Macmillan, 1965.
School of the Sun [*Primera memoria*]. Translated by Elaine Kerrigan. New York: Pantheon, 1963.
"A Wounded Generation." Translated by A. Gordon Ferguson. *The Nation* 201 (29 November 1965): 420–24.

II. A Selected Bibliography of Works Consulted

Adams, Mildred. "Two Adolescents Bent on Evil." *New York Times Book Review,* 21 April 1963, p. 4.
Alborg, Juan Luis. *Hora actual de la novela española.* Madrid: Taurus, 1958.
"Ana María Matute." *Revista de actualidades, artes y letras* 9 (16 January 1960): 8–9.
Aragonés, Juan Emilio. "Ultima promoción." *Ateneo,* no. 64 (1954), p. 40.
B. de C. "Crónica del 'Premio Planeta 1954.'" *Correo literario* 5 (November 1954).

Baeza, Fernando. "El año literario en España." *Indice* 10 (December 1955–January 1956): 29.

Baquero Goyanes, Mariano. "La novela española de 1939 a 1953." *Cuadernos hispanoamericanos* 24 (July 1955): 81–95.

Berger, Yves. "L'Espagne de Ana María Matute." *La Nouvelle Revue Française* 9 (1 May 1961): 896–901.

Berrettini, Celia. "Ana María Matute, la novelista pintora." *Cuadernos hispanoamericanos* 48 (December 1961): 405–12.

———. "Los niños en la obra de Ana María Matute." *Universidad de Antioquia*, no. 153 (April–May–June 1963), pp. 314–21.

Bosch, Rafael. Review of *Historias de la Artámila* by Ana María Matute. *Books Abroad* 36 (Summer 1962): 303.

———. Review of *Los soldados lloran de noche* by Ana María Matute. *Revista hispánica moderna* 30 (July–October 1964): 309.

C. L. A. Review of *Primera memoria* by Ana María Matute. *Punta Europa*, no. 51 (March 1960), pp. 100–101.

Camus, Albert. *Le Mythe de Sisyphe*. Edition augmentée. Paris: Gallimard, 1943.

Cano, José Luis. "La novela española actual." *Revista nacional de cultura* 20 (November–December 1957): 18–22.

———. Review of *Los Abel* by Ana María Matute. *Insula* 4 (15 February 1949): 5.

———. Review of *Los hijos muertos* by Ana María Matute. *Insula* 14 (15 January 1959): 8–9.

———. Review of *Pequeño teatro* by Ana María Matute. *Insula* 10 (15 March 1955): 6.

———. Review of *Primera memoria* by Ana María Matute. *Insula* 15 (April 1960): 8–9.

———. Review of *Los soldados lloran de noche* by Ana María Matute. *Insula* 19 (15 September 1964): 8–9.

Castellet, José María. "Ana María Matute, Premio 'Planeta' 1954." *Revista* 3 (21 October 1954): 6.

———. "Anaquel: El pequeño teatro del mundo." *Correo literario* 5, no. 9 (January 1955).

———. "La joven generación española y los problemas de la patria." *Revista nacional de cultura* 24 (September–December 1961): 149–64.

———. *Notas sobre literatura española contemporánea*. Barcelona: Ediciones Laye, 1955.

———. "La novela española, quince años después (1942–1957)."

Cuadernos del congreso por la libertad de la cultura, no. 33 (November–December 1958), pp. 48–52.

———. "Panorama de los jóvenes: la novela." *Correo literario* 5 (December 1954).

Castillo, L. "Entrevista con Ana María Matute." *Ateneo* 2 (14 September 1953): 19.

Castro y Delgado, Juan de. Review of *Fiesta al noroeste* and *Los soldados lloran de noche* by Ana María Matute. *Razón y fe* 173 (March 1966): 328.

Cienfuegos, Sebastián. "Le Roman en Espagne." Translated by Pierre Gamarra. *Europe,* nos. 345–46 (January–February 1958): 17–29.

Cirlot, J. E. *A Dictionary of Symbols.* Translated by Jack Sage. New York: Philosophical Library, 1962.

Coindreau, Maurice Edgar. "Homenaje a los jóvenes novelistas españoles." *Cuadernos del congreso por la libertad de la cultura,* no. 33 (November–December 1958), pp. 44–47.

———. "La joven literatura española." *Cuadernos del congreso por la libertad de la cultura,* no. 24 (May–June 1957), pp. 39–43.

Couffon, Claude. "Una joven novelista española: Ana María Matute." *Cuadernos del congreso por la libertad de la cultura,* no. 54 (November 1961), pp. 52–55.

Crusat, José. Review of *Los niños tontos* by Ana María Matute. *Revista de actualidades, artes y letras* 6 (28 December 1957–3 January 1958): 8.

Crusat, P. Review of *El tiempo* by Ana María Matute. *Insula* 13 (15 March 1958): 8.

"De la cruz a la letra." *Ateneo* 3 (15 January 1954): 23.

Duque, Aquilino. Review of *Los hijos muertos* by Ana María Matute. *Cuadernos hispanoamericanos* 42 (April 1960): 148–53.

Entrambasaguas, Joaquín de. Review of *En esta tierra* by Ana María Matute. *Revista de literatura* 9 (January–June 1956): 186–87.

Fernández-Almagro, M. Review of *Los hijos muertos* by Ana María Matute. *ABC,* 7 May 1959.

———. Review of *Primera memoria* by Ana María Matute. *ABC,* 14 April 1960.

Fuentes, Victor. "Notas sobre el mundo novelesco de Ana María Matute." *Revista nacional de cultura* 25 (September–October 1963): 83–88.

García-Luengo, Eusebio. "Premio Café Gijón, 1952: impresiones de un miembro del jurado." *Indice* 7 (15 May 1952): 3.

————. Review of *Los Abel* and *Fiesta al noroeste* by Ana María Matute. *Indice* 8 (30 October 1953).

García Viñó, M. *Novela española actual*. Madrid: Ediciones Guadarrama, 1967.

Gich, Juan. "*Los Abel*, primera novela." *Cuadernos hispanoamericanos*, no. 7 (January–February 1949), pp. 219–20.

González Ruano, César. "Una tarde con Ana María Matute." *Correo literario* 5 (November 1954).

Gracia Ifach, María de. Review of *Los niños tontos* by Ana María Matute. *Insula* 12 (15 May 1957): 7.

Griffin, David. Review of *El tiempo* by Ana María Matute. *Books Abroad* 32 (Autumn 1958): 432.

Group, William J. "Contemporary Spanish Literary and Intellectual Life." *Modern Language Journal* 45 (April 1961): 156–60.

Gullón, Ricardo. "España, 1958." *Asomante* 14 (July–September 1958): 67–74.

————. "España, 1960." *Asomante* 16 (January–March 1960): 52–56.

————. "The Modern Spanish Novel." Translated by Douglass M. Rogers. *Texas Quarterly* 4 (Spring 1961): 79–96.

Harth, Dorothy E. Review of *En esta tierra* by Ana María Matute. *Books Abroad* 31 (Summer 1957): 298.

Hornedo, Rafael María de, S.I. "El mundo novelesco de Ana María Matute." *Razón y fe* 162 (July–December 1960): 329–46.

Hoyos, Antonio de. *Ocho escritores actuales*. Murcia: Aula de cultura, 1954.

J. M. C. "Entrevista con Ana María Matute." *Insula* 15, no. 160 (March 1960): 4.

J. V. P. Review of *Primera memoria* by Ana María Matute. *Archivum* 10 (January–December 1960): 456–58.

Jones, Margaret W. "Antipathetic Fallacy: The Hostile World of Ana María Matute's Novels." *Kentucky Foreign Language Quarterly* 13 (Supplement 1967): 5–16.

————. "Religious Motifs and Biblical Allusions in the Works of Ana María Matute." *Hispania* 51 (September 1968): 416–23.

Jones, Willis Knapp. "Recent Novels of Spain: 1936–56." *Hispania* 40 (September 1957): 303–11.

Keller, Daniel S. Review of *Tres y un sueño* by Ana María Matute. *Books Abroad* 36 (Winter 1962): 61–62.

Livingstone, Leon. "Interior Duplication and the Problem of Form in the Modern Spanish Novel." *Publications of the Modern Language Association of America* 73 (September 1958): 393–406.

Lundkvist, Artur. "Mellan Kain och Abel." *Bonniers Litterära Magasin* 31 (January 1962): 692–99.

Mallo, Jerónimo. "Caracterización y valor del 'tremendismo' en la novela española contemporánea." *Hispania* 39 (March 1956): 49–55.

Marill, Réné Albérès. *L'Aventure intellectuelle du XXᵉ Siècle: Panorama des Littératures Européennes.* Paris: Editions Albin Michel, 1958.

————. *Histoire du Roman moderne.* Paris: Editions Albin Michel, 1962.

————; Bastide, Roger; Bazin, Louis; Couffon, Claude; and others. *Les Littératures contemporaines à travers le Monde.* Paris: Librairie Hachette, 1961.

Marra-López, José Ramón. "Novelas y cuentos." *Insula* 17 (May 1962): 4.

————. Review of *Primera memoria* by Ana María Matute. *Cuadernos del congreso por la libertad de la cultura,* no. 43 (July–August 1960), pp. 119–20.

Martínez, Palacio, Javier. "Una trilogía novelística de Ana María Matute." *Insula* 20 (February 1964): 6–7.

Martino, E. Review of *Historias de la Artámila* by Ana María Matute. *Humanidades* 32 (May–August 1962): 301–2.

————. "El último Nadal." *Humanidades* 12 (May–August 1960): 197–200.

Mendilow, Adam Abraham. *Time and the Novel.* London: P. Neville, 1952.

Micó Buchón, J. L. "Prosa española, siglo XX." *Humanidades* 9, no. 18 (1957): 203–29.

Molist Pol, E. Review of *Pequeño teatro* by Ana María Matute. *Revista* 3 (23–29 December 1954): 10.

Morales, Rafael. "Buen estilo narrativo y logrados personajes en *Pequeño teatro.*" *Ateneo* 4 (January 1955): 77.

Murciano, Carlos. "Notas al paso: narraciones." *Punta Europa,* nos. 66–67 (June–July 1961), p. 136.

————. Review of *Los hijos muertos* by Ana María Matute. *Punta Europa,* no. 41 (May 1959), pp. 142–43.

Narvión, Pilar. "Viaje al mundo interior de Ana María Matute." *Ateneo* 3 (1 November 1954): 6.

Nora, Eugenio G. de. *La novela española contemporánea (1927–1960).* Vol. 2. Madrid: Editorial Gredos, 1962.

"Noticias bibliográficas: *Tres y un sueño*," *Razón y fe* 164 (July–December 1961): 140.

Nuñez, Antonio. "Encuentro con Ana María Matute." *Insula* 20 (February 1965): 7.

Olmos García, Francisco. "La novela y los novelistas españoles de hoy." *Cuadernos americanos* 129 (July–August 1963): 211–37.

P. L. A. Review of *Los niños tontos* by Ana María Matute. *Quaderni ibero-americani* 4 (1961): 96.

P. N. "El Premio 'Planeta' 1954 para Ana María Matute." *Ateneo* 3 (15 October 1954): 7.

Pageard, Robert. "Romanciers et Conteurs Espagnols actuels." *Mercure de France* 327 (1 March 1957): 530–37.

Pérez Minik, Domingo. *Novelistas españoles de los siglos XIX y XX*. Madrid: Guadarrama, 1956.

Pilar Palomo, María del. Review of *Historias de la Artámila* by Ana María Matute. *Revista de literatura* 20 (July–December 1961): 450–51.

"Premio Café Gijón, 1952." *Revista*, no. 2 (14 April 1952), p. 10.

Prjevalinsky Ferrer, Olga. "Las novelistas españolas de hoy." *Cuadernos americanos* 118 (September–October 1961): 211–23.

"¿Qué libros han influído más en su vida?" *Revista de actualidades, artes y letras* 8 (18 April 1959): 10.

Q[uinto], J[osé] M[aría] de. "El mundo de Ana María Matute." *Revista española* 1, no. 3 (September–October 1953): 337–41.

R. G. Review of *Fiesta al noroeste* by Ana María Matute. *Insula* 8 (15 July 1953): 6.

R. M. "Ana María Matute, Premio Nadal 1959." *Revista de actualidades, artes y letras* 9 (9 January 1960): 6.

Review of *Los niños tontos* by Ana María Matute. *Insula* 12 (15 February 1957): 14.

Rodríguez Luis, Julio. Review of *El tiempo* by Ana María Matute. *La torre* 7 (April–June 1959): 164–70.

Sainz de Robles, Federico Carlos. *La novela española en el siglo XX*. Madrid: Pegaso, 1957.

——. *Panorama literario*. 2 vols. Madrid: Colección El Grifón, 1954–1955.

Sassone, Helena. "Hacia una interpretación de la novela española." *Revista nacional de cultura* 13 (September–December 1960): 43–57.

Serrano Poncela, S. "La novela española contemporánea." *La torre* 1 (April–June 1953): 105–8.

Slonim, Marc; Lin Yutang; Rimanelli, Giose; and Torres-Rioseco, Arturo. *Perspectives: Recent Literature of Russia, China, Italy, and Spain.* Washington: Library of Congress, 1961.

Sordo, Enrique. "Una gran novela." *Revista de actualidades, artes y letras* 7 (20–26 December 1958): 28.

——. "El mundo interior de Ana María Matute." *Revista de actualidades, artes y letras* 6 (21–27 December 1957): 38.

——. "Panorama de la joven literatura española." *Revista de actualidades, artes y letras* 5 (19–25 July 1956): 14.

——. Review of *En esta tierra* by Ana María Matute. *Revista de actualidades, artes y letras* 4 (24–30 November 1955): 14.

——. Review of *Los niños tontos* by Ana María Matute. *Revista de actualidades, artes y letras* 6 (22–28 June 1957): 14.

——. Review of *Primera memoria* by Ana María Matute. *Revista Gran Vía de actualidades, artes y letras* 9 (23 April 1960): 14.

Spens, Willy de. Review of *El tiempo* by Ana María Matute. *Nouvelle Revue Française* 18 (1 July 1960): 135–36.

Talamas, Carlos. Review of *Fiesta al noroeste* by Ana María Matute. *Correo literario* 4, no. 72 (15 May 1953): 7.

Torrente Ballester, Gonzalo. *Panorama de la literatura española contemporánea.* Madrid: Ediciones Guadarrama, 1956.

Van-Praag Chantraine, André and Jacqueline. "Ana María Matute ou la Recherche de l'Enfer Perdu." *Synthèses: Revue Internationale* 17 (April 1962): 59–78.

Vilanova, Antonio. Review of *Los mercaderes* by Ana María Matute. *Destino* (4 October 1964), pp. 57–59.

——. "Los premios de la crítica 1958." *Papeles de Son Armadans* 12 (May 1959): 226–31.

Volmane, Vera. "Ana María Matute." *Les Nouvelles Littéraires* 41 (30 May 1963): 10.

Winecoff, Janet. "Style and Solitude in the Works of Ana María Matute." *Hispania* 49 (March 1966): 61–69.

Wythe, George. "The World of Ana María Matute." *Books Abroad* 40, no. 1 (Winter 1966): 17–28.

Notes

Introduction

[1] The following sources have provided biographical information: a mimeographed "Autobiografía de Ana María Matute," furnished by the author; Ana María Matute, untitled essay in *El autor enjuicia su obra* (Madrid, 1966), pp. 141–45; idem, "A Wounded Generation," translated by A. Gordon Ferguson, *The Nation* 201 (29 November 1965): 420–24; George Wythe, "The World of Ana María Matute," *Books Abroad* 40, no. 1 (Winter 1966): 17–28; Claude Couffon, "Una joven novelista española: Ana María Matute," *Cuadernos del congreso por la libertad de la cultura*, no. 54 (November 1961), pp. 52–55; Antonio de Hoyos, *Ocho escritores actuales* (Murcia, 1954), p. 156.

[2] Matute, "A Wounded Generation," p. 420.

[3] Ibid.

[4] Eugenio G. de Nora, *La novela española contemporánea* (1927–1960) 2, pt. 2 (Madrid, 1962): 289.

[5] Marc Slonim and others, *Perspectives: Recent Literature of Russia, China, Italy, and Spain* (Washington, 1961), p. 50.

[6] José María Castellet, "La novela española, quince años después (1942–1957)," *Cuadernos del congreso por la libertad de la cultura*, no. 33 (November–December 1958), p. 52.

[7] The frequent use of the word "world" in studies dealing with Matute's literature affirms the uniqueness of her conception of life: Rafael María de Hornedo, S.I., "El mundo novelesco de Ana María Matute," *Razón y fe* 162 (July–December 1960): 329–46; J[osé] M[aría] de Q[uinto], "El mundo de Ana María Matute," *Revista española* 1, no. 3 (September–October 1953): 337–41; Wythe, "World of Ana María Matute," pp. 17–28; Victor Fuentes, "Notas sobre el mundo novelesco de Ana María Matute," *Revista nacional de cultura* 25 (September–October 1963): 83–88.

1. The Works of Ana María Matute

[1] For bibliographic information on Ana María Matute's works, see pp. 123–24.

[2] For remarks on the committee's reception of *Los Abel*, see: Juan Luis Alborg, *Hora actual de la novela española* (Madrid, 1958), p. 181; and Olga Prjevalinsky Ferrer, "Las novelistas españolas de hoy," *Cuadernos americanos* 118 (September–October 1961): 223.

[3] José Luis Cano, review of *Los Abel*, *Insula* 4 (15 February 1949): 5.

[4] She won the Premio Café Gijón for this work. All references here are to the third edition (Barcelona, 1963).

[5] Rafael María de Hornedo, S.I., "El mundo novelesco de Ana María Matute," *Razón y fe* 162 (July–December 1960): 346.

[6] Carlos Talamas, review of *Fiesta al noroeste*, *Correo literario* 4, no. 72 (15 May 1953): 7.

[7] Matute, "Autocrítica de *Fiesta al noroeste*," *Correo literario* 3, no. 46 (15 April 1952): 5.

[8] Ibid.

[9] José María Castellet, "Ana María Matute, Premio 'Planeta' 1954," *Revista* 3 (21 October 1954): 6.

[10] "Pequeño teatro fue mi primera novela escrita 'en serio.' La escribí después de pasar una temporada en el pueblecito vasco de Zumaya. La Oiquixa de mi libro es una mezcla, mitad realidad mitad fantasia, de Zumaya." In Claude Couffon, "Una joven novelista española: Ana María Matute," *Cuadernos del congreso por la libertad de la cultura*, no. 54 (November 1961), pp. 54–55.

[11] José María Castellet, "Anaquel: El pequeño teatro del mundo," *Correo literario* 5, no. 9 (January 1955).

[12] José Luis Cano, review of *Pequeño teatro*, *Insula* 10 (15 March 1955): 6.

[13] Alborg, *Hora actual*, pp. 183–84.

[14] Ibid., p. 189.

[15] Ibid., p. 185.

[16] A[ntonio] V[ilanova], "Los premios de la crítica 1958: *Los hijos muertos* de Ana María Matute," *Papeles de Son Armadans* 12 (May 1959): 227.

[17] "El tiempo" first appeared as "La pequeña vida," *La novela del sábado* 1, no. 11 (n.d.): 5–64.

[18] Vilanova, "Los premios," p. 228.

[19] Ibid., p. 229.

[20] Rafael Bosch, review of *Historias de la Artámila, Books Abroad* 36 (Summer 1962): 303.

2. The World of Childhood

[1] Matute has also written several books for children: *El país de la pizarra* (Barcelona, 1956); *Paulina, el mundo y las estrellas* (Barcelona, 1960); *El saltamontes verde* (Barcelona, 1960); *Caballito loco* (Barcelona, 1962); and *El polizón del "Ulises"* (Barcelona, 1965). These works will not be studied here.

[2] *Los hijos muertos* is an exeption: Miguel's childhood takes place during the Civil War. Since the novel does not comprise childhood alone but deals extensively with the later periods of life, Matute makes liberal use of contemporary events.

[3] Claude Couffon, "Una joven novelista española: Ana María Matute," *Cuadernos del congreso por la libertad de la cultura*, no. 54 (November 1961), pp. 52–55.

[4] "Hay un paisaje y unos hombres que 'se meten' en mis libros, casi sin darme yo misma cuenta. Es la tierra de Castilla, concretamente de la sierra de Cameros, donde teníamos la casa y las tierras de mi madre." Ibid., p. 55.

[5] She uses these very words in *A la mitad del camino*, p. 81, and *Fiesta al noroeste*, p. 17, and implies the same in *Los niños tontos*, p. 84, and *Pequeño teatro*, p. 88.

[6] Eugenio G. de Nora, *La novela española contemporánea* (1927–1960) 2, pt. 2 (Madrid, 1962) notes that the themes of solitude and escape are basic to Matute's literature (p. 292, footnote 6).

[7] Other works expand this idea. Valba Abel describes the attitude of the townspeople toward actors: "Era asombroso ver a aquellas mujeres de la aldea, siempre de gesto avinagrado y lleno de desesperanza, acudir con sillas y bancos, llevando de la mano a sus hijos niños. . . . Por lo visto también conocían la ilusión de cuando en cuando" (*Los Abel*, p. 102). Sitting behind his friend Dingo during the show offered by the travelling puppeteers, Juan notes that "la nuca de su amigo se le ofrecía negra, con una inmovilidad de alucinado, de ensueño. Fué la última vez que le vio niño, abrasado de ilusión"

(*Fiesta al noroeste*, p. 92). For further references to travelling players, actors, circus performers, puppeteers, marionettes, toy theaters, disguises, and costumes, see *Los Abel, El arrepentido* ("Navidad para Carnavalito"), *Historias de la Artámila* ("El incendio," "Don Payasito"), *Los niños tontos* ("El jorobado"), *Pequeño teatro, Primera memoria, Tres y un sueño* ("La oveja negra"), *A la mitad del camino* ("Siempre los cómicos," "Panchito").

[8] Pedro's alienation leads naturally to the attendant theme of escape, symbolized by the word *alas*: "A veces, se sentía tan próximo y unido a todo ello, y otras, en cambio, le inundaba la sensación de lejanía, y parecía como si le brotaran unas absurdas alas que le llevaban aparte. . . . Ah!, si no hubiera sido por culpa de aquellas alas que inesperadamente le remontaban del suelo y le apartaban de todo, Pedro hubiera continuado siendo un niño feliz. Pedro, sin saber cómo, se quedaba de pronto tan lejos, tan indiferente" (*El tiempo*, pp. 15–16).

[9] Specific passages which furnish Matute's definition of the child's world emphasize a strange admixture of reality and fantasy in which sensorial awareness permits new discoveries and also provides the door to another dimension: "Es falso que el mundo infantil sea confuso, lleno de formas vagas y de suave poesía. La poesía vive en el niño auténtica y pura: es siempre una poesía vigorosa, de colores recios y contornos bien definidos" (*A la mitad . . .* , p. 199). "Un caótico país de abigarrados e indisciplinados colores, donde caben infinidad de islas brillantes, lagunas rojas, costas con perfil humano, oscuros acantilados donde se estrella el mar en una sinfonía siempre evocadora, nunca desacorde con la imaginación. . . . Claro está que habría que añadir a todo eso el sonsonequete de la tabla de multiplicar, el chirriar de la tiza en la pizarra, . . . el crujir de los zapatos nuevos, la ceniza del habano de papá. . . . Y también rondan aquellas playas unas azules siluetas indefinidas que tal vez representan el miedo a la noche, y una movible hilera de insectos multicolores cuya sola vista produce idéntica sensación a la experimentada junto a los hermanos menores. Y aquellas campanadas súbitas, inesperadas, que resuenan desde sabe Dios dónde y se espera bobamente poderlas contemplar grabadas en el mismo cielo" (*El tiempo*, pp. 115–16).

In the recollection of a childhood incident, Matute discards specific time references in favor of the memory associated with a sensorial image: "(Recuerdo que yo mordía la cadenilla de la medalla y que sentía en el paladar un gusto de metal raramente frío. Y se oía el canto crujiente de las cigarras entre la hierba del prado)" (*Historias* . . . , p. 59).

[10] In the child's world there is a general disregard of specific time and setting. Because of this nontemporal conception, the reader must surmise that this episode refers to the Civil War, though Matute never states this openly.

[11] References to water are another clever device to avoid mentioning time and to further enhance the idea of immobility in childhood. Flowing water is a generally accepted symbol for the passage of time: a river, for example, may stand for "the irreversible passage of time and, in consequence, for a sense of loss and oblivion." J. E. Cirlot, *A Dictionary of Symbols*, translated by Jack Sage (New York, 1962), p. 262.

[12] *Hora actual de la novela española* (Madrid, 1958), p. 190.

[13] The theme of death has been noted by one critic in the following statement: "El mundo rico y emotivo de nuestra escritora se ve sorprendido y dominado por el tema de la muerte." Antonio de Hoyos, *Ocho escritores actuales* (Murcia, 1954), p. 159.

[14] It can be assumed that Matute has transferred her personal feelings to the special child in some way, and that in the exaltation of the imaginative powers of childhood, we may find a decisive factor in her own youth. Discussions of her life repeatedly emphasize the importance of her childhood, and certain factors closely parallel those of the children in her stories. In an untitled essay in *El autor enjuicia su obra* (Madrid, 1966), p. 141, she states that through her imagination, she created a separate, magic world for herself: "Yo fui lo que podría llamarse una niña feliz, hasta los diez años. Ciertamente, vivía refugiada en lo que podía llamar 'país' propio al que difícilmente daba entrada a los demás. Tenía mi teatro de marionetas, mi muñeco negro, mis libros de cuentos." The outbreak of the Civil War changed her existence; this could be compared with the reality which breaks into the fictional child's happy life. As an escape mechanism, she forged herself a make-believe world with the stories and plays she wrote and her puppets and dolls (see Couffon, "Una joven novelista," p. 54). Probably her treatment of childhood is directly inspired by her own experiences during this age. In the magic world she describes, in the happiness of the children, she may be recalling her own childhood; the clash of reality and fantasy may well be an unconscious manifestation of the effect of the Civil War on her own life.

3. The World of Adolescence

[1] The solitude which plagues the characters in Ana María Matute's works is one of the most basic themes in her production, yet one which has not often drawn the critics' attention. Her work is a study in different phases of loneliness, from simple physical separation to active estrangement; other essential themes (such as time, death, the Cain and Abel motif) are drawn from or contribute directly to the pattern of loneliness. For further comments on this, see Eugenio G. de Nora, *La novela española contemporánea* (1927–1960) 2, pt. 2, p. 292; Janet Winecoff, in "Style and Solitude in the Works of Ana María Matute," *Hispania* 49 (March 1966): 61–69, treats this theme extensively.

[2] One common denominator for the adolescents is the holdover of some of their childhood innocence and purity. Zazu's one preoccupation is to retain the candid, pure look in her eyes (*Pequeño teatro*, p. 30); Matia notes in one of her parenthetical observations about early adolescence, "Y, sin embargo, qué limpios éramos, todavía" (*Primera memoria*, p. 23). These childlike qualities will fade as the adolescent becomes more acquainted with the adult world.

[3] This forms one part of the Cain and Abel motif, which will be discussed in chapter 5.

[4] This is also a variation on the reflection motif, for the adolescent sees himself mirrored in others.

[5] Many of the adolescents' thoughts and actions are reminiscent of existentialist theories (loneliness, the wish for freedom, a desire for self-definition and then commitment, alienation, an acknowledgment of the absurdity of life and the needlessness of human existence). Matute does not, however, present a consistently existentialist viewpoint, nor are her heroes existentialists in the complete sense of the word.

[6] That is, in *Los soldados lloran de noche*. Following the classic pattern, Jeza's death has deprived Marta of her happiness; Manuel's natural reticence and lack of interest in social convention show his indifference to society. Thus both are estranged or unhappy in some way. After a lengthy reconstruction of Marta's life with Jeza, they willingly sacrifice themselves by futilely resisting the oncoming *nacionales*. They have committed themselves irrevocably and have carried out their commitment successfully, but the price is death. Bear also sacrifices himself for another's cause (*La trampa*).

[7] Ricardo Gullón sees in the use of animals the symbol "of the

person struggling to be free in the face of the society which destroys him." Gullón, "The Modern Spanish Novel," translated by Douglass M. Rogers, *Texas Quarterly* 4 (Spring 1961): 94. Rafael María de Hornedo, S.I., "El mundo novelesco de Ana María Matute," *Razón y fe* 162 (July–December 1960): 335–36, also mentions the numerous adolescent rebellions, which he ascribes to "anticonformismo social."

4. Adulthood

[1] J. M. C., "Entrevista con Ana María Matute," *Insula* 15, no. 160 (March 1960): 4.

[2] Pablo Barral becomes an adult during an uprising he is leading: victory does not hold even momentary satisfaction. With a terrible feeling of solitude in the midst of the crowd and haunted by an intuition of his personal defeat, Pablo symbolically ends his own adolescence by murdering all traces of his past: "Cuando, cara a la pared, disparó a la espalda del sacerdote, mató en su corazón al párroco que le hizo tantas veces la señal de la Cruz en la frente, allí en la aldea. Cuando mató a la mujer del dueño del molino, de ojos negros y turbios, mataba en su corazón a la mujer del herrero. Cuando mató al hijo de Lucas Fernán, el alcalde, un muchacho delgado y blanco que estudiaba Filosofía, se mató a sí mismo en su corazón" (*En esta tierra,* pp. 199–200).

[3] Further examples of this can be found in *En esta tierra,* which uses the counterpoint technique of alternating Pablo's solitude and disillusion with descriptions of the mob (p. 199); and in *Los hijos muertos,* which presents "la masa, en su más absoluta soledad, codo con codo" (p. 306).

[4] *Los hijos muertos* bears this theory out. The book compares the adolescent and the adult Daniel, shuttling between past and present, at times confusing them, always ironically torturing the protagonist who evokes these memories in the first place. Isabel, too, is involved in this kind of reconstruction. Many characters in *La trampa* are also obsessed with the past.

[5] Although Diego Herrera's optimism may seem to be an exception, it is not. At the end of the novel he is forced to give in, as the impossibility of his hopes for the prison camp and the death of his symbolic son mark the beginning of his pessimism. I will treat this more fully later.

[6] Albert Camus, *Le Mythe de Sisyphe,* edition augmentée (Paris, 1943), p. 18. Another tantalizing point of contact is Camus's statement concerning the loss of hope for a promised land. These, of course, are the very words which describe the situation of Pablo Barral (*En esta tierra*).

[7] Camus, *Mythe de Sisyphe,* p. 48.

[8] The staring eye, imparting connotations of accusation or guilt feelings, is an artistic reminder of Daniel's sense of failure. Other examples may be seen in recollections of some episodes of his adolescence, overlayed, of course, with his sense of defeat (pp. 165–66).

[9] *La trampa* also reinforces adult pessimism through the idea of the inevitable, although, like *Primera memoria* and *Los hijos muertos,* the characters' foreknowledge of tragedy justifiably supplies the necessary atmosphere. There are symbols, for example, referring to well-ordered machines and the impossibility of stopping them once set in motion. Many of these have to do with the actual murder plans, but the last-minute retraction of Mario's and Bear's gratuitous act do indeed suggest a certain fatality. Some allusions to this aspect may be seen in the following phrases: "Sólo sé que de ahora en adelante hay algo fatal en todos nuestros gestos" (p. 129); "Tío Borja, aún sin sospecharlo, ha entrado en el juego, está ya apresado en el engranaje" (p. 67); Mario is "nacido para perder" (p. 49).

[10] The author's growing concern with hypocrisy and egotism, and her special manner of presenting and "combatting" these problems are discussed in the last chapter.

[11] After failing to find satisfaction in the revolution, Pablo commits continual suicide with his image in the mirror: "Pablo dispararía contra los espejos doblando su final, anticipadamente, para gozar y sufrir, a un tiempo, con el espectáculo de su destrucción" (*En esta tierra,* p. 238). The old man in "El arrepentido" commits suicide because he has lived the wrong kind of life (p. 20); Juan Medinao's mother hangs herself when she learns that her husband's mistress (a servant in the house) has borne a child (*Fiesta al noroeste*).

[12] Pablo is modeled after a pattern which Matute uses again and again; he is an expanded version of the schoolmaster, whose drunkenness helps him to forget his shattered idealism. This will be treated later.

[13] Claude Couffon, "Una joven novelista española: Ana María Matute," *Cuadernos del congreso por la libertad de la cultura,* no. 54 (November 1961), p. 52.

[14] In essence, Eloy describes the life of a man from the moment of birth in the middle of the fields, where his mother ties his umbilical cord with a lace from her *alpargata*. At first he remains with her, tied to her back; later he is locked at home during the day while his mother works in the fields. He finally marries after "un amor breve y sangriento que se lleva a cabo tras una era." His wife, old before her time, will give birth to a child who will repeat the same cycle.

[15] Characteristics common to the lower classes of *En esta tierra* and "El maestro" (*El arrepentido*) and other works.

[16] Couffon, "Una joven novelista," p. 52.

5. Style and Artistic Vision

[1] Ana María Matute, *Doce historias de la Artámila*, ed. Manuel Durán and Gloria Durán (New York, 1965), p. ix.

[2] J. M. C., "Entrevista con Ana María Matute," *Insula* 15, no. 160 (March 1960): 4.

[3] Antonio Nuñez, "Encuentro con Ana María Matute," *Insula* 20 (February 1965): 7.

[4] Claude Couffon, in "Una joven novelista española: Ana María Matute," *Cuadernos del congreso por la libertad de la cultura*, no. 54 (November 1961), pp. 52–55, provides a wealth of material on this subject. On p. 52, Matute says, "Muchos de estos campesinos hombres, mujeres y niños que allí conocí, fueron después personajes de mis libros. . . . Aquellas mujeres que iban a arar con sus hijos atados a la espalda, aquel recién nacido tumbado en una manta, al resguardo de un viejo paraguas abierto, junto a la comida y el vino, en el huequecillo de piedras de la era, bajo un sol redondo y cruel. A-quellos dos muchachos que vendieron el caballo para poder sembrar la tierra, e iban arrastrando entre los dos el arado, inclinados bajo la soga, surcos adelante."

[5] The novelist herself has verified the note of protest in *Pequeño teatro*: "Pienso que en este libro el impulso más fuerte fue denunciar la 'falsa caridad' que me exasperaba." Couffon, "Una joven novelista," pp. 54–55.

[6] Ana María Matute, "Yo no he venido a traer la paz . . . ," *Cuadernos del congreso por la libertad de la cultura*, no. 67 (December 1962), pp. 53–63.

[7] For further comment on this aspect of Matute's work, see my

article "Religious Motifs and Biblical Allusions in the Works of Ana María Matute," *Hispania* 51 (September 1968): 416–23.

[8] Critics invariably mention the Cain-Abel motif as a key theme. For further discussion of this point, see: George Wythe, "The World of Ana María Matute," *Books Abroad* 40, no. 1 (Winter 1966): 24–25; Victor Fuentes, "Notas sobre el mundo novelesco de Ana María Matute," *Revista nacional de cultura* 25 (September–October 1963): 84; Artur Lundkvist, "Mellan Kain och Abel," *Bonniers Litterära Magasin* 31 (January 1962): 692–99.

[9] Couffon, "Una joven novelista," p. 55.

[10] Ibid.

[11] Ibid.

[12] Ibid., p. 52.

[13] For further study of the way in which style enhances theme, especially in *Fiesta al noroeste*, see Janet Winecoff, "Style and Solitude in the Works of Ana María Matute," *Hispania* 49 (March 1966): 61–69.

[14] J. E. Cirlot, *A Dictionary of Symbols*, translated by Jack Sage (New York, 1962), p. 104.

[15] *Primera memoria* is filled with nature images of this kind. For a more detailed study of this in *Primera memoria* and other works, see my article, "Antipathetic Fallacy: The Hostile World of Ana María Matute's Novels," *Kentucky Foreign Language Quarterly* 13 (Supplement 1967): 5–16.

[16] Brief biographies mention her studies in both art and music; see Antonio de Hoyos, *Ocho escritores actuales* (Murcia, 1954), p. 156.

[17] Celia Berrettini, "Ana María Matute, la novelista pintora," *Cuadernos hispanoamericanos* 48 (December 1961): 405–12.

Index

[*Characters are listed by first name.*]

Design by Jonathan Greene

Set in Rudolf Ruzicka's Linotype Fairfield
with F. W. Goudy's Deepdene
used for display

Composed, printed & bound
by the Kingsport Press